GRACIOUS LIVING

To my sweet neighbor Sonja —
Blessings !
Margaret

GRACIOUS LIVING

Creating a culture of honor, love,
and compassion

Margaret Allen

Carpenter's Son Publishing

Gracious Living

©2020 by Margaret Allen

Published by Carpenter's Son Publishing, Franklin, Tennessee

Published in association with Larry Carpenter
of Christian Book Services, LLC
www.christianbookservices.com

Published in association with Ivey Beckman Enterprises
iveyharringtonbeckman.com.

Scripture taken from the NEW AMERICAN STANDARD BIBLE®, Copyright © 1960,1962,1963,1968,1971,1972,1973,1975,1977,1995 by The Lockman Foundation. Used by permission.

Scripture taken from *The Message*. Copyright © 1993, 1994, 1995, 1996, 2000, 2001, 2002. Used by permission of NavPress Publishing Group

The stories in *Gracious Living* are true; however, some names and identifying details have been changed for privacy.

Edited by Ivey Harrington Beckman

Cover Design Michael Palana @mykeycreative

Interior Design by Suzanne Lawing

Printed in the United States of America

978-1-952025-08-2

To my lifelong mentor, Judy Rothell
You waited forty years for this book.
Thank you for believing, dear friend,
and for loving me so well.

Contents

Part Three: Walking Your Path

ACKNOWLEDGMENTS

If you see a turtle on a fence post, you know it didn't get there on its own. I would like to thank the following people for their help with *Gracious Living*. Without them, this book would have never gotten off the ground.

My husband, Andy, for modeling graciousness, wisdom, and goodness. I love you!

My beautiful children, Miranda, Nicole, Brooke, and Cooper. Your sweet spirits are the greatest joys in my life. Thank you for inspiring me and cheering me on. I hope I make you proud.

My loving friends who encouraged me to write and push through all my doubts and insecurities: Joanne Beasley, Tracy Newman, Lacie Burger, Christi Martinelli, Amy Kelm, Jennifer Morris, and Cheryl Batzing.

The Stanford Chi Alpha, and especially the young women who urged me to record my stories and have continued to pray for this book: Victoria Gonzales, Adrienne Ivey, Heather Aholt, Jessica Reed, Brittany Foerster.

Jeremy and Debora Anderson, for speaking prophetically in my life and modeling a compelling, winsome walk with God.

Priscilla Welsh, for your insightful writing in the "Meaningful Dialogue" sections.

Special thanks to Ivey Harrington Beckman, my editor, writing coach, and wise sage. You demonstrate graciousness in every way. Thank you for making me feel safe in the writing process.

FOREWORD

By Debora Anderson, Chi Alpha Campus Missionary

A few years ago, I had a dream. In the dream my friend, Margaret Allen, wrote a book titled *Gracious Living*. The next morning, that dream came to my mind, vibrant and full of God's presence. I knew God was showing me what was in His heart, and I had to share this prophetic dream with Margaret. Before I scheduled a visit with my friend, I had someone create a tote bag with the words *Gracious Living* printed on it. It represented the lifestyle Margaret lives and champions with great conviction.

Margaret and I initially connected because we shared a desire to see the kingdom of heaven envelop university campuses. Over time, we've cultivated a close friendship. Margaret has consistently challenged me to elevate my thinking, take ordinary things and make them excellent, find the gold in every person and circumstance, be ever mindful of God's presence, and see every relationship as an opportunity to add value to that individual. She has added value to me through God-induced words and actions, propelling me to walk with a more vibrant understanding of God's excellency and reflect His nature to those around me.

I once heard Margaret speak at a leadership conference. She stirred up something in that room that could not be shaken or ignored. She called us to a higher standard of living—to reflect God's heart through embracing excellence in all we do, treating our families and our work with attentive care and intentional devotion.

As Colossians 3:23 states, "Whatever you do, work heartily, as for the Lord and not for men." After hearing Margaret speak from her heart that day, we all felt empowered to up our game—for our assignments in life are not mediocre; they are high callings. We were encouraged to look at all that we put our hands to and ask, "Does my effort reflect the heart and nature of God the Father?"

When you spend time with Margaret, you can't escape thought-provoking questions as she partners with the Holy Spirit to bring wisdom, truth, perspective, and encouragement that move you to dream bigger and live a magnanimous, divinely gracious life. Margaret's life demonstrates that when you are dedicated to going the extra mile with your family, work, and ministry, it's not about what you receive, or how high you climb; it's about displaying the nature of our Maker.

As you read *Gracious Living*, know that you are receiving from someone who lives out the message of gracious living; therefore, there is an anointing and responsibility to impart the gold you find on these pages. Margaret has left strong impressions of God's kingdom in all those blessed to know her. My prayer is that you are emboldened to do the same as you read *Gracious Living*. Posture your heart to receive and be transformed by God's message—because this book began in His heart.

PART ONE

Reaching In

"So, here's what I want you to do, God helping you:
Take your everyday life—your sleeping, eating, going-to-work, and walking-around life—and place it before
God as an offering. Embracing what God does for you
is the best thing you can do for him. …fix your attention
on God. You'll be changed from the inside out."

ROMANS 12:1-2

1

Women Who Create

"Those who sow in tears shall reap with joyful shouting."
PSALM 126:5

We are creating atmospheres around us all the time—the good, the lovely, and alas, the downright ugly. One day, I spotted a friend of mine driving next to me on the freeway. She's a successful young professional, a great listener, and known for her compassion and thoughtfulness. Just as I was about to honk and wave, another car cut her off. My friend laid on the horn and gave that driver the one-finger wave! My mouth dropped open—but not as much as hers when she glanced over and saw me. We both shrugged our shoulders and laughed. I still tease her about that freeway-wave.

But let's get real. We've all been there. We've generated negativity on the freeway, at the grocery store, in the workplace and at school, in restaurants—and certainly in our homes.

Sure, we can laugh about our ungracious behavior, but that doesn't change the truth: it's not pretty.

But with God's help, we can choose to change the atmospheres around us. As women cherished by God, we can create beautiful, gracious environments filled with honor, love, and compassion.

We begin by first believing just how much life-giving grace flows through us as God's beloved daughters. We are vibrant, compelling, and creative beings! By God's design, each of us brings a unique touch, flavor, and impact on every situation. We create love or hate, peace or strife, blessing or cursing, chaos or order. It's our choice.

And here's the golden nugget: *what if the secret of personal flourishing stems from the daily choice of compassion, excellence, and altruism toward others? Simply filling our everyday, walking-around lives with kindness that draws people to Him?*

Years ago, when I was a campus minister at Stanford University, I met a young guy at an on-campus worship service. The moment I laid eyes on him, God gave me the words to say: "Hey man, I don't know you, but I feel like God is showing me this about you…"

I immediately had his attention because the message God gave me was spot-on. On campus, he was a well-known, outspoken atheist. He asked if he could meet with me later that week, and I responded, "Sure—if you will read the Book of Ephesians to prepare for our discussion."

This young guy came to my office later that week and would not shut up about the Book of Ecclesiastes. He kept quoting Ecclesiastes and saying how much it spoke truth to him and so on.

Finally, I asked, "Why are you so interested in Ecclesiastes?" He replied, "As a philosophy major, I'm shocked at how much truth and wisdom is in this book. I had no idea the Bible talked about these things! I'm impressed you knew to have me read it!"

I laughed and replied, "Dude, I told you to read *Ephesians*, not Ecclesiastes. As a pragmatist, I would never tell anyone to read Ecclesiastes. I don't even understand what half that book is about!"

After we both had a good laugh, I concluded, "God knew what you needed to hear. He took my scant human logic and changed the wording just for you."

My friends, gracious behavior is not a huge undertaking. It's simply living out our day-to-day lives under the hand of God, fixing our attention on Him. It's praying for His will throughout every moment. And, sometimes, that happens in spite of our words and actions! God takes our feeble attempts—our little lunch of bread and fish—and multiplies it to be the perfect solution for someone.

Speaking of Ecclesiastes, I love 10:12. "Words from the mouth of a wise man are gracious, while the lips of a fool consume him." Now, that's clarity! A wise woman's words are gracious. They comfort, guide, and sustain. They purchase good feelings. On the flip side, the lips of a fool speak ungracious and offensive words to others. And those caustic words are like slow-drip poison in the woman speaking them. Again, it's a matter of choice!

Let's bring this ancient wisdom from Solomon alongside a commentary on Jesus, written by one of His contemporaries: "And all were speaking well of Him, and wondering at the gracious words which were falling from His lips; and they were saying, "Is this not Joseph's son?" (Luke 4:22)

I could stop quoting right there, and we would all say, "Well, isn't that special!" But for integrity's sake, check out

Luke 4:23-30. The quick rundown is that Jesus stated some uncomfortable truths. The people who were awed by the gracious behavior of a carpenter's son were suddenly mad as hell and tried to throw Him off a cliff. His response? He walked away while they raged.

In the next scene, the authority of Jesus amazed a new group of listeners. And maybe that's a snippet of gracious living. If you can lovingly speak what God is saying in a given situation, you might look like Jesus. Of course, you may get a mixture of reactions. People who hear your words may marvel at the beauty and grace of them. However, you might tick some folks off when you speak the truth.

You see, gracious living isn't about some smarmy, marshmallow niceness. It's about being genuinely kind and compassionate, creating life by speaking what you hear God saying.

The Softening of Motherhood

Living a gracious life hasn't always been my thing. When launching a campus ministry at Stanford University, I didn't grasp the power or potential of the grace available to me as a daughter of God. I didn't know I had blessings to give. Life was something that just happened to me. I assumed whatever transpired in my daily life must be God's will. And I believed I was just a wee bit less valuable than everyone around me, clawing and fighting for stuff was a way of life for me.

In my first twelve years as a campus chaplain at Stanford University, I approached my students like a drill sergeant. My goal was to challenge them, disrupt their comfortable Christianity, and plug them into my organizational puzzle. I relentlessly pushed my students toward discipline and order. We studied and memorized Scripture, journaled, battled sin, read the classics, and held campus-wide events to share the gospel. I had verses that backed up every obligation and requirement I laid down. My measuring stick was always nearby: have I prayed enough, witnessed enough, memorized enough, done enough?

At the end of those twelve years, I was exhausted from trying to do everything right. I was apathetic and disillusioned. I felt most believers I knew didn't take Christianity as seriously as I did. I was bored with the treadmill of doing. Honestly, I believed God let me down. I thought, *Surely, there has to be more to the Christian walk than this! Why don't I hear God's voice more, and why does my spiritual life feel like sweat work?*

To soften my heart for graciousness, it took stepping away from the work world and into motherhood. Ten years later, I had four precious children at home under the age of seven— Miranda, Nicole, Brooke, and Cooper. Time melted into a sea of playdates and diapers, mountainous loads of laundry, cuddling in bed with four little people, much joy, and little sleep.

While my husband was traveling worldwide with Apple, I was home, replacing the noise of the world with tiny peanut-butter-smeared voices. The early childhood years wreaked havoc with my previous images of order and control. Days could pass without time for a shower or a sit-down meal. Some days, I would've paid $100 for an hour alone at Starbucks!

But motherhood softened me. So many women I've talked with say the same thing. Exiting the dog-eat-dog work world and entering a more gentle, cooperative season at home changes women. The rough edges come off; intuition and thoughtfulness blossom. I noticed that after I had children, I was more sensitive to violence in movies and television. I was nurturing and shielding young, vulnerable humans, and I didn't want to hear cursing and yelling. Call it hormones if you want, but sappy commercials brought me to tears, as did country-western songs about momma. When my children were present, I became mindful of the behaviors I was modeling. I was beginning to realize that, inside all of us, there is a little child who wants to be treated gently.

I'll be frank though; I did experience an identity crisis in those early days as a stay-at-home mom. *If I was not a hardcore, cutting-edge campus minister, who was I? Was I just a mom in a minivan? And if so, so what?*

But slowly, I realized my identity doesn't rest on what I do or how I look but on what Jesus has done for me. I'm a child of the King—a beautiful, unconditionally loved, blood-bought daughter of God Almighty! I'm the apple of His eye, His choice possession, His friend, His beloved. I'm forgiven and accepted. God has given me every spiritual blessing, and I have all that I need for life and godliness. I am enough!

In time, I came to see myself differently. Yes, I was a mom in a long line of minivans headed to elementary school, but my vehicle had glorious light shooting into the heavens. Praise, worship, and glory pulsated throughout it. My minivan bubbled with prayer, revelation, and joy.

Sometimes, I would smile to think I looked so typical—so mundane—when I was brimming with the power that raised Jesus from the grave! In the sacred sanctuary of my tan minivan, I embraced a life-giving truth: We create grace when we focus on giving it to those around us. We create grace when fulfilling our God-given purposes makes the world a better place.

As my identity became anchored in Christ, I grew in graciousness. I was an ambassador representing the King. My everyday life of carpools, playdates, laundry, and sporting events was one opportunity after another to represent Jesus! I discovered the power of blessing others through speaking encouragement and truth. I reveled in the beauty of what I was creating in my family and life.

Sure, there were plenty of setbacks—angry words, impatience, weariness, selfishness, pride, worldliness. But God Himself is gracious and kind, isn't He? He just kept meeting me, loving me. God spoke truth, revelation, and insight into my spirit. He brought me alongside amazing people who modeled passion, integrity, and grace. God taught me the power of choice—and the magical, gracious love found in motherhood.

The Seasoning of Secular Friends

Motherhood softened my heart to love more graciously, but non-Christians seasoned me for living with everyday grace.

I became a campus minister when I was twenty-three. I ministered with inner-city youth in Houston before moving to California to work at Stanford. Wonderful Christian roommates marked my college years, and most of my free time was spent doing campus ministry. When church is your thing, and ministry is your job, it's easy to become isolated from non-Christians.

When I ventured outside my Christian circle, I was somewhat surprised to discover that most of the moms and neighbors around me were delightful, kindhearted people. They often possessed more emotional maturity and compassion than women I'd known in church. (Could it be that some women focus on biblical literacy and certain forms of morality, while others spend that time in more socially diverse settings, unwittingly building emotional IQ?)

Let's be frank, we've all tangled with mean-spirited, small-minded, judgmental chicks in church. My secular friends confronted attitudes I carried around like sledgehammers. They challenged how I prioritized some virtues but not others. Isn't that what Jesus did when He said, "Hypocrite! For you clean the outside of the cup and the dish, but inside they are full of robbery and self-indulgence" (Matthew 23:25). Those doses of reality, though humbling, were freeing and invigorating!

My non-churched friends modeled far more sophisticated hospitality than what I had experienced in our church fellowship hall on Sunday nights. They seasoned me for the nit and grit of life. They taught me that the tenderness of love far surpasses the sharpness of judgment.

Learning that lesson in graciousness has made a world of difference in my life, time and time again. A friend once confided that she and her husband had brought another couple into their bedroom. She thought switching things up with different sexual partners would bring excitement back to their marriage. I looked at her like a deer caught in headlights. All I could think to say was, "How's that working for you?" She burst into tears, and I just held her. There are times too delicate for a sermon or a verse of the day, and I was glad that my non-churched friends had seasoned me with the emotional IQ to simply love and embrace with grace.

The Awakening of the Holy Spirit

The softening of motherhood and the seasoning of non-churched friends were lifechanging gifts of grace. However, my encounters with the Holy Spirit fully awakened me to a crystal-clear vision of gracious living. Every morning, before my kids were up, I would bring my weary heart to God. I hungered for Him in Scripture, not for teaching material, but for sustenance. Knowing the long and tedious day ahead of me, I clung to His every word.

I've known plenty of dry days at the feet of Jesus when my prayers echoed like a hollow-drum monologue. But those sunrise meetings became encounters with a Living Presence. I would hear missionaries talk about God speaking to them, but they weren't from my church background, and I found their statements suspect. But still, I wanted to believe they were true.

As days passed, my fellowship grew sweeter with God, and I was emboldened to ask for more:

> *God, I want everything You have for me! I've languished on little drips and drabs, impressions, maybe an answered prayer or a verse that stands out. Lord, I know You didn't die for just this! I know You want more for me. I want to experience deep joy and peacefulness, hear Your voice, know when You are here and when You pull back. I want intimate friendship with You, Holy Spirit.*

My cry for more of His presence continued for months. Friends who seemed to walk closely with Christ would tell me, "Margaret, you're so close! Don't give up on a greater encounter with Him!"

One Sunday morning, when my husband, Andy, had taken the kids to Tahoe for a fun weekend with Dad, I decided to visit a small church I'd heard about. When I arrived, I thought, *Uh-oh, I'm in a SNL comedy skit!* I mean, it was whack-a-doodle. The congregation wasn't singing; they were groaning, each person shouting their own thing. Before I could beat a path to the exit, someone put me in a prayer line. Every person came before a young man speaking what he felt the Spirit saying to that individual. Then, each person fell to the ground! I was in the line, praying, *Lord, help this young man to not base his spirituality on whether someone falls or not, because You know I'm not going to act like that!*

When it was my turn, the young man looked at me with the sweetest brown eyes and said, "There's a grace on you." And I fell to the ground—out cold. When I woke up, it was as if I were covered head to toe in the love of God. I was belly laughing, and I could not help it.

Someone finally picked me up and sent me out behind the church with two young gals, probably seventeen years old. They both wore huge hoop earrings, red lipstick, and smacked gum while explaining some of what had just happened to me. They recited and explained 1 Corinthians 12, 13, and 14. I thought, *I've spoken at conferences to more than 7,000 people. I have a seminary degree. I've been a minister at one of the world's leading universities, and yet I'm being schooled on the Holy Spirit by two teenagers.* I felt like a baby, an infant in the kingdom of God.

After that experience, my sunrise times with the Holy Spirit brimmed with sweetness, not sweat and silence. God's Spirit ministered to me—speaking, guiding, revealing truth, awakening an intimate friendship I'd never before known. My heart for people changed too. I had a bounce in my step, an easiness and joyfulness that emanated from my times with God. Often, I was surprised to find that I knew things from the Holy Spirit that I couldn't have known otherwise.

It made no logical sense to me at that time, but my experience in that whack-a-doodle church shifted something for me. It was as if I'd been searching for a radio station, and I finally tuned in to the right frequency. God was coming in loud and clear! I felt closer to Christ. I knew what the Holy Spirit was saying whereas before I only had vague impressions.

During one of my sunrise prayers, I distinctly remember saying, *God, You don't have to make sense to me. I'm releasing this idol of understanding, of being in control, of forcing You to fit into my theology. God, please astound me, surprise me, open me up to greater truths.* And, good gracious, did He answer that prayer!

How about you, my friend? Does God have to make sense to you? Do you hunger for a more profound presence in your life? Are you willing to suspend judgment on what seems far out? Isn't that what Jesus was asking us to do in the parable of the Good Samaritan? What human logic exists in stopping for a stranger? We can't approach an upside-down kingdom with human reasoning. The first will be last doesn't make sense, but the flip-flop is astounding!

I've discovered a tremendous adventure awaits in letting go and leaning into the Holy Spirit. Gracious living calls me out of a logic-driven life and into a Spirit-inspired life! Isaiah 49:6 is one of my life verses.

> "It is too small a thing that You should be My
> Servant to raise up the tribes of Jacob and to re-
> store the preserved ones of Israel; I will also make
> You a light of the nations, so that My salvation
> may reach to the end of the earth."

If our primary calling is to be a light to nations so that salvation through Christ will reach the ends of the earth, we have life-giving, grace-filled choices to make every day. I've come to some conclusions about why we should choose graciousness and compassion in everyday life—and by doing so, share the love of God in a world filled with hostility and disharmony.

• **The status-quo isn't working.** Not being kind, gracious, generous, and compassionate is failing. There's too much friction. There's too much focus on self. Being unkind repels people. It's petty, cynical, corrosive, and small. It's unfulfilling and stressful. (I think it's even harmful on a cellular level because it creates stress.) And if you and I don't share how Christ has set us free, we're living in "less than" mode. Less than our potential, less than our destiny, and far less than God's grand plan for us as His beloved daughters!

• **Being gracious is good for us.** When we are gracious, kind, generous, and compassionate to those around us, we're more vibrant and energized. We gain a sense of fulfilling our destiny and making the world a better place. It's a fun, adventurous, and robust way to live.

• **We represent Jesus to the world.** We should view them through His eyes. Jesus sees us as precious, beloved children. When we embrace our God-given commission to represent Jesus to the world, we can see people as the precious treasures they are. And when we do that, being gracious, kind, generous, and compassionate become life-giving choices. In his book, *Translating God*, Shawn Bolz puts viewing others the way Jesus views them this way: "See what God sees, hear what God hears, and speak what God speaks so we can all love the way God loves."[1] What a beautiful picture of the vision for gracious choices!

A Gracious Living Experiment

I began my years at Stanford acting like a drill sergeant; I ended them as a love bug. After ten rejuvenating and enlightening years off, rearing my precious rowdy crew of four, I returned to Stanford with a new purpose. Working with Chi Alpha, a campus ministry, I decided to try a gracious-living experiment.

Realizing I am creating environments all the time, I chose to love my students unconditionally. I chose to speak and model love. I gave them admiration, honor, my time—and vulnerability. I caught them doing good things and celebrated those things with them both privately and publicly.

I accepted my students and never judged them or measured them by my ideals or standards. I trusted the Holy Spirit to speak truth to them. I shared the lessons I was learning and the beauty I observed in the world around me. I left room for them to make their own decisions.

Before every mentoring session, I asked the Lord for a prophetic word or picture for that student. I asked for exhilarating "Ah-ha!" moments to usher in revelation and freedom. More than anything else, I determined that they would learn from me how cherished and celebrated they are in the eyes of God.

How did my gracious-living experiment end? After five years of practicing love, acceptance, generosity, and gracious non-judgment, the results were indisputable. As I finished my time at Stanford, a friend asked why I was leaving my role. Besides needing to do more writing, I replied, "I kind of feel like I'm half-assing it. All I do is show up and love people." Her response? She smiled and said, "Margaret, isn't that exactly what Jesus did?"

It almost felt unfair how much love and honor I received from students during my final months at Stanford. One gal I mentored, a surfer from Southern California who had become a Christian at Stanford, shared what had touched her the most about me. She simply said, "You never tried to fix me, Margaret. You just loved me and spoke life into me way more than correcting me."

Another student, a gal studying engineering, reflected that I helped her learn how God sees her. "I don't have to live in condemnation or shame," she said. "I can go before God as a daughter, knowing that I am fully loved. It's because of the truth you planted, Margaret, that I can receive the freedom to walk in God's grace. He is not disappointed in me. I now see myself as He sees me: forgiven, redeemed, and clean; one He delights in and enjoys; one with access to grace that He doesn't revoke."

Gracious living works miracles, my friend! It shapes us into better people; it empowers the people around us to flourish. We are made to create loving and honoring space for one another. And whose example are we following? God's! Scripture tells us, "We love, because He first loved us. ... The Lord is compassionate and gracious, slow to anger and abounding in lovingkindness" (1 John 4:19; Psalm 103:8).

When we embrace gracious living, we are mirroring God! He smiles; we smile. He is gracious; we are gracious. He doesn't hold a grudge; we don't hold a grudge. He is patient and kind. He doesn't cling to a wrong suffered. He bears all things, hopes all things, and endures all things. And we are empowered to do likewise! We sync our heartbeats with the heart of God. We value what He values. And that's a beautiful way to live.

So, as God's daughters, let's embrace graciousness. Let's choose to create atmospheres of grace. Let's live graciously for His glory—and in the process, become stunningly beautiful women who shine like beacons and change the world—one car in traffic, one minivan, one neighbor at a time.

Meaningful Dialogue

1. Describe an experience that softened you. What did God reveal to you during that time?

2. What negative environments could you change to create positive spaces?

3. When have you felt someone was trying to fix you? Have you caught yourself trying to fix others or change their behavior?

4. Where do you need the Holy Spirit to come alive in your life? You can ask for the Spirit's help, knowing that His voice will lovingly bring you closer to God.

5. Are you holding anything back from God? Is there any area of your life that you are afraid to hear what He has to say?

Declarations for Gracious Living

As the eyes of servants look to their master, so my eyes look to You, O God! (Psalms 123:2)

The Lord leads me in the way I should go. (Isaiah 48:17)

I am brimming with righteousness and peace and joy in the Holy Spirit! (Romans 14:17)

2

A Touch of Self-Grace

"I will give thanks to You for I am fearfully and
wonderfully made; Wonderful are your works,
and my soul knows it very well."

PSALM 139:14

If you want to embrace gracious living, you must start with
yourself. Self-grace begins with recognizing and silencing
those nattering voices inside your head: the harsh voice of
self-criticism, the raspy voices of envy and perceived lack, and
the painfilled voice of rejection.

These days, the perfection pressure exerted on a woman
is exhausting. She must look hip and have her stuff together
all of the time. Her career must be fabulous. If she's a mom,
her offspring must appear happy, well-adjusted, and casually
stylish. Her home must be neat; meals healthy, organic, and
gluten-free. You get the idea.

What conversations natter in a woman's head when she can't measure up to that perfection scale? She may say berating things to herself that she would never utter to a girlfriend. It doesn't have to be that way.

One morning, as I was sitting under the summer flowers of my crepe myrtle trees, with a cup of coffee in hand, my friend Lacie texted me:

> *"Guess who did NOT see their kindergartener start school today?"*

The text was followed by the girl emoji with hand raised and three crying faces, along with the following:

> *"I took Lauren to her third-grade class, and by the time I got to Bennett's room to hug him, take pictures, and tell him to have the best day ever, he was already in class. Door shut. All the new kindergarten parents were outside teary-eyed. When I saw I missed Bennett's first day—the biggest milestone of all milestones—I stood teary with all the others!"*

So, did this precious young mom berate herself? Did she dive into frantic activity to prove her worth as a mother and mitigate the guilt of her mistake? Did she jealously lash out because the other mothers shared a once-in-a-lifetime moment she missed? Did Lacie lament that other mothers had more time than she did? Thankfully, no! Instead, she concluded her text with advice for other moms out there:

> *"My nugget of wisdom is to have your husband take the oldest to class so you can be at kinder drop-off for all your babies. And you better believe tomorrow I'm going to school thirty minutes early with Bennett!"*

Here's what I love about my friend's response: She owned her mistake, grieved the loss, and then laughed about it. She didn't let it define her. Instead, Lacie made appropriate adjustments and shared what she learned. She didn't allow guilt and shame to wreak havoc on her identity. She didn't wallow in feelings of envy or rejection. Instead, Lacie embraced the propelling power of self-grace. And as a daughter of God, you are worthy of the freedom that self-grace can give you. You, too, can silence those disparaging voices inside your head.

Silencing the Harsh Voice of Self-Criticism

Many of us listen to thoughts that are more abrasive than any words we would ever say aloud. We continually try to shrug off a nagging sense of shame and inadequacy. Where do we most often see self-criticism with clarity? In the mirror.

"Mirror, mirror on the wall." What we say to the mirror is a true reflection of receiving love and worth from God—or rejecting it. I used to look in my mirror with disdain. I'd tsk over my freckles and wrinkles, sigh at my low-hanging boobs, and fat-shame myself over my not-so-flat belly. I even wrote "Wide-Load Maggie" on a picture of myself that wasn't flattering and stuck it on my refrigerator!

Two truths helped me get out of that destructive thought cycle:

• **God doesn't make ugly.** I'm a beautiful creation, and I shouldn't criticize what God has made.

• **As a woman thinks in her heart, so she is.** If in my heart I think I'm not good enough, I won't be. And if, in my heart I think I'm beautiful, then I will be. You see, the woman who thinks she can't—and the woman who thinks she can—are right.

How did I change my mirror image? I started blessing my mirror. That's right, I would smile at myself first of all, and then I would say:

> *God, I thank You that I am fearfully and wonder-*
> *fully made. Thank You for these freckles and wrin-*
> *kles. They are unique to my face, and they remind*
> *me of all the days You've brought me through.*
> *God, thank You for these saggy boobs that have*
> *nursed four children. Thank You for this belly that*
> *makes me soft to hug. I bless my belly and hips to*
> *make me feel round and sexy, and I also bless my*
> *eating and exercise to be precisely what my body*
> *needs. God, I bless my entire body in Jesus name.*
> *Show me how to care for my physical being, how to*
> *nurture it, cherish it, strengthen it. And thank You,*
> *God, for blessing every cell, every muscle, every*
> *tendon, every organ. Amen*

If this wording is too over the top for you, simply smile at yourself every time you look in the mirror and say, *God loves me.* You'll feel better inside, and you might look better on the outside too!

You see, Christ's love has revolutionized my thinking. When I mess up, I don't mentally say, *Ugh, Margaret, you are such a screwup!* I wouldn't say that to a friend, nor would you. Instead, I treat myself with the same love and compassion as I would a girlfriend. Sometimes, the most kind and gracious women have no grace for themselves because they think others are worthy, but they are not. What we say in our heads verifies if we've received His message—or not. I'm telling you, grasping the heart of God's message is a game-changer!

If women are around church for any length of time, the tendency is to yawn and say, *I know; Jesus loves me, uh-huh.* But when we bask in His heart toward us, relishing our value and honor as daughters of the King of all kings, everything—and I mean everything—changes, including self-talk.

My friend, gracious living flows from a deeply personal and satisfying experience with God's love. Sure, we can labor to become more gracious, but it overflows naturally from a love encounter with Christ.

Do the conversations in your head sound like someone who is deeply loved and secure? Is your self-talk filled with compassion and gentleness? Would you hope your daughters talk about themselves in similar ways? Small changes produce significant results. Thinking of yourself and talking to yourself with affection and appreciation may seem insignificant, but it cascades into a more gracious environment all around. Silencing the harsh voice of self-criticism and speaking to yourself with grace is sunshine for your soul, my friend. You'll feel the warmth—and so will others.

Silencing the Raspy Whispers of Envy and Lack

Sometimes, those inner voices can be so subtle and insidious we're oblivious to them—until attitudes and actions rear their ugly heads. When you're tempted to dwell on thoughts of envy and lack, it indicates you're running on a dry tank. Think about the last time you were envious; someone had something you wanted. Maybe it was a certain level of success, a specific accomplishment, a relationship—or perhaps it was thick, wavy hair and a flat stomach.

No matter the type of envy, it's like a flashing red light on the dashboard signaling a problem. What's the glitch? We often don't have a clear picture of who we are and our destiny. The only reason someone else's future looks enticing is that we don't have a crystal-clear vision of where God is taking us.

Once we get clear on who we are, then we can celebrate the victories of others.

Envy and lack both rely on scarcity thinking. There are only so many pieces of the pie. We fear there's not enough to go around.

I'll never forget the moment I realized lack was more of a mindset than a reality. I was on a ski vacation in Utah. The Snowbird ski area boasted of extreme skiing in steep terrain. Restaurants featured gourmet everything and lodging was world-class. To top it all off, fresh powder covered the slopes.

The T-shirts in Utah read, "No Friends on a Powder Day," and it was true that day with my husband and me. Andy was skiing the advanced double-black-diamond area, while I surfed the intermediate runs on my snowboard.

Toward the end of the day, I headed for a black-diamond run. Quickly, I was in terrain steeper than anything I'd ever imagined. I was alone in an area, and it screamed beyond my skill level. Frustrated by my fear, I cautiously worked my way down the slope before quitting for the day.

I immediately headed to the hot tub where several people were soaking and laughingly said, "I hope one of you brought me a beer!" They replied, "We're Mormon!"

More disappointment! I trudged back to my room in a bad mood. All I could feel was lack. I wasn't a daredevil on my snowboard. I didn't like the minimalist architecture of our lodge. My husband was probably having the best day ever, and I couldn't even find a beer!

When all those feelings pummeled me at once, I started laughing and thought, *Devil, you are a liar!* I recalled Psalm 34:10: "Even young lions lack and suffer hunger, but they that wait upon the Lord lack no good thing." I laughed at how absurd my situation was. Then a genuinely gracious message sounded in my head:

> *Maggie, you're at one the most extreme mountains in the United States, staying in a gorgeous lodge, and you're healthy enough at fifty to snowboard black-diamond slopes! Your hunky husband is going to be back soon, and you're going to enjoy a gourmet, organic meal in the scenic, snow-packed mountains. Be grateful for who you are and where you are, girl!*

Lack is a mindset and not a reality. Those who love us surround us—and yet we can feel alone. We can gush with accomplishment and success and still feel the weight of failure. Transformation comes only through the renewing processes of soaking in God's Word and in prayer, which silence the raspy whispers of envy and lack.

Now when I begin to feel that I'm not enough or that my circumstances fall short, I remind myself that I lack no good thing. Christ poured out all that we need for life and godliness. He loves me and has good plans for my life. Genuine graciousness launches from His transformational work in my heart and mind and spills out onto every relationship.

Silencing the Painfilled Voice of Rejection

A girlfriend once confessed to me about an encounter with God at a weekend retreat. Coming across Proverbs 28:1a, "The wicked run even when no one is chasing them," she sensed God nudging her. She realized she felt rejected even when no one was rejecting her and judged when no one was judging her. She tearfully continued that she often felt people didn't like her, when in fact they did. It was as if God pulled the curtain back so that she could plainly see the source of many heartaches—the churlish voice of rejection.

My friend was at a weekend retreat, investing time with God when He nudged her, and she cried to Him, *Lord, please heal my heart! Help me to see the truth about who I am in You.* God then touched that sore spot and transformed her. Several hours passed as she cried and experienced the healing work of the Holy Spirit. She exclaimed to me, "It's like scales fell from my eyes!" She embraced God's love and affection for her, and He silenced the inner voice of rejection. The change was evident: she carried new ease, confidence, and a genuine interest in others. Being loved, and knowing that we are loved, is transformative, my friend.

Women often struggle with feeling like rejected orphans. But we are not orphans. Nor do shame and rejection hold rightful places in our personalities because of Christ. Why? Because we are accepted and cherished. In Christ, we are forgiven and set free from all sin and shame. God adopted us into His family. These are truths from Scripture, but we stumble in believing them. When the Bible proclaims, "We love because He first loved us," it's banking on our vibrant experience with God's love. It assumes that our behavior and attitudes dramatically shifted when we encountered His graciousness.

We can be gracious and kind toward ourselves because of God's love and acceptance of us. Embracing this truth results in peaceful, personal security. When we are secure in who God says we are, we don't jostle and shove for status. We stop competing and striving. We rest. Without all that energy going toward proving our worth, we are freed to care for others.

When we walk in the love of God, realizing our worth and acceptance, we don't sweat the small stuff. This is a refreshing trait of healthy, gracious Christians. When things go wrong, like the dishwasher flooding those beautiful hardwood floors, traffic derailing a flight, or friends canceling long standing plans, it's okay. Chaos may exist on the outside, but calm reigns on the inside.

I frequently sing the *Frozen* song, "Let it Go," when I sense myself tensing up over some obstacle, difficulty, or disappointment. I am confident that even in the paper cuts of life, God's promises bring forth good. And in the big pitfalls, our inner reservoir of God's love, bubbling up from the friendship of the Holy Spirit, sustains us through every trial.

> *"For I am convinced that neither death, nor life,*
> *nor angels, nor principalities, nor things present,*
> *nor things to come, nor powers, nor height nor*
> *depth, nor any other created thing, will be able to*
> *separate us from the love of God, which is in Christ*
> *Jesus our Lord"* (Romans 8:38-39).

God's love is enough whether our struggle takes place in a hospital bed, government housing, an Ivy-League classroom, or a grand estate. We each tap into His love and acceptance to help us through the details of life. One of my favorite Texas axioms shouts, "When God closes one door, He always opens another, but sometimes it's hell in the hallway!" In Christ, we have the resources to handle whatever comes our way, even if it is hell in the hallway.

Hearing the Bright and True Voices

Here's what I do to ensure the conversations inside my head burn bright and true:

• **I review encouragement often.** If I receive an email, text, or letter that lifts my countenance, reveals truth, or demonstrates my place in the world, I don't stuff it in the back of a drawer or lose it in my 7,000 emails! Instead, I treasure it front and center. I either file it in my Encouragement Journal or save it in my Encouragement email folder. Things that are said about me, prophetic words spoken to me, dreams that seem significant, special thank-you notes, and ways I've spoken into someone's life are stored and reviewed often.

When God applies a Scripture to me in a compelling way, I don't just underline it and forget about it. Rather, I take a few moments to write it out, along with how God pressed it into my mind. I want to be like Samuel, described as "never letting God's word fall to the ground" (1 Samuel 3:19). I catch and treasure what God says to me because it is always reliable!

• **I elicit feedback.** When I hit my fifties, my changing hormones and health led me into a year of anxiety and depression. I spent a weekend at a lake cabin to sit at the Lord's feet and get clarity about why, for the first time in my life, I was struggling with anxiety and sadness. I asked God, *Is it my hormones changing with menopause? Is my thyroid function off? Is it part of Celiac disease? Is it because my precious daughters are leaving for college and our house feels so quiet? Is it because I'm considering retirement from campus ministry? Does my marriage need attention?*

I sensed God say to me, *Yes, Maggie (He calls me Maggie in tender moments). Yes, it's all that and more.* I felt validated in that moment and peaceful. Isn't it funny how one word from God changes everything? I'm so glad I could go to Him and receive help. Then I could determine where to apply the guidance, nurture, and compassion.

Not only did I elicit feedback from God, I also turned to those closest to me. I confessed to my family and a few best girlfriends that I felt lost, anxious, and sad—and that I needed reassurance from them. I needed hugs and affection. I needed them nearby and on-call when experiencing an especially dark day. One of the most beautiful things to come out of this were affirmations from loved ones. I asked each of my close friends and family members to list twenty-five of their favorite things about me as I was struggling to find one. I treasure these lists and review them often to this day!

• **I practice gratitude.** My practice comprises three simple activities every day: I take a few minutes to turn my affection toward God. Some days, I have more time, but at a minimum, I spend five minutes loving Him and celebrating His friendship in my life. It can simply be turning my face upward toward the sun for a few moments; dancing when a song comes on; or cherishing the sweetness of a moment in prayer.

Every day I also jot down three things for which I'm grateful. It's my private list, so if my gratitude that day is coffee, sex, and sunshine, I don't have to explain or sanitize my answer.

• **Lastly, and this one takes a wee bit more effort, I send an encouraging text or email to someone.** Whoever comes to mind, I take that as a sign from God. I send them a Bible verse, tell them why I'm grateful for them, or share what I'm praying about for them. You might ask, "How does this help you, Margaret?" If I consistently speak life over others, it will stand out as incongruent if I speak poorly to myself. If I'm better to others, I will be better to myself, plain and simple.

Wherever you are in life my friend (a student striving to discover your path, a young mom juggling multiple kids and obligations, a woman feeling stuck in her career, or someone in a challenging relationship), I encourage you to seek a love encounter with Jesus Christ. May it be so satisfying and authentic that you are changed from the inside out. You can hold all kinds of pleasant thoughts about Jesus in your mind. For real life change though, you must give your life to Him, believing that He is Lord and Savior and turning away from a self-directed life full of negative voices. The first step toward gracious living is to accept the grace of God. To take that step, simply pray a prayer similar to this one:

> *Lord Jesus, I'm giving You control over my life because I believe You are God. You love me and want to save me, heal me, deliver me, and make me whole. I trust You to come into my life, take away my sin, and give me a new spirit. I receive Your love displayed through Jesus Christ on the cross. With Your Holy Spirit living inside of me, I promise to love You and follow You all the days of my life. Amen*

When you allow God to wrap His grace-filled arms around you and then choose to follow His lead and hug yourself, everything changes. You are free to love others and embrace them with grace. You become a messenger of mercy. You become a shining beacon who draws others to Jesus, a woman of grace full of hope and truth—a real beauty.

Meaningful Dialogue

1. Which areas of your life are the hardest to show yourself grace?

2. What Scriptures could you speak, or even memorize, that strengthen your identity in Christ? What truths about you, as a believer, shine in Scripture?

3. What are lies, whispered by the enemy, that hurt or impede your walk with God? How can you rebuke that line of thinking and replace it with truth?

4. What phrases and self-talk can you practice in your everyday thoughts and conversations to bring about positive change?

5. Whether you have been around church for years or are new to the God scene, what are ways you can wholeheartedly enter into the love of Jesus?

Declarations for Gracious Living

Whoever calls on the name of the Lord will be saved, healed, delivered, and made whole. (Romans 10:13)

God has loved me with an everlasting love. (Jeremiah 31:3)

I take every thought captive to the obedience of Christ, and I destroy every lofty thing raised against the knowledge of God. (2 Corinthians 10:5)

3

The Soul of Friendship

*"The soul of Jonathan was knit to the soul of David,
and Jonathan loved him as himself."*
1 SAMUEL 18:1B

My concept of friendship expanded while I was on a trip to Europe. For years, I dreamed of going to the Christmas markets in Germany. Once you see pictures of the *Christkindlmarkts* held throughout Germany and much of Europe, you'll add a visit to your bucket list! Some of these markets have existed for hundreds of years. Booths and lights line town squares, and local artists sell their goods, along with food and wine to warm the winter chill.

I can only describe it as sheer joy the first time I walked onto *Marienplatz* in Munich. Snow was lightly falling on the booths. My daughters were on Christmas break from college, and together we were enjoying every bit of the wintery experience. A lesson in friendship came from, of all places, a

Biergarten! As we were walking through the marketplace with our guide, he pointed to a large table of older men wearing traditional leather Bavarian overalls. Each drank from a unique beer stein, unlike the clear mugs everyone else had.

"Look!" our guide said. "That's an old *Stammtisch* (German for Regulars Table). Those men meet every Wednesday at this time at that table. They've met for over forty years, and some of their fathers met together before them. They store their beer steins in lockers at the garden so that they drink from their own mugs each week."

As an American—fiercely independent, isolated, and often alone—I found the concept of a *Stammtisch* astonishing: same time, same table, same people for years—even decades. When I think about the ingredients that make a *Stammtisch* work, I'm mystified—the level of commitment, the perpetual curiosity about one another that spans years, the enjoyment of each person for who they are, the saying *no* to many new and shiny things to say *yes* to a *Stammtisch*. Wow!

I found similar friendship scenarios throughout Europe. In Dublin, I had a conversation with almost every cab driver that went like this:

Me: *"Hi, are you from Dublin?*

Old Guy Cabbie: *Aye, well, what do you think? Of course, I'm from Dublin! Why would anyone leave here?*

Me: *Do you still stay in touch with friends from high school?*

Old Guy Cabbie: *Aye, well, what do you think? Of course, I do! Lord, girl, we all meet up for a pint every week. Don't you's?"*

It was impossible to explain to him that it takes fifteen back-and-forth texts to find a day *next month* that my three closest friends and I can all meet. How could I defend that

I've never even been inside the homes of some of my friends? How could I extol the American commitment to independence over community when it clearly throws up roadblocks to close relationships?

As Americans, we are cutting ourselves way short where friendships are concerned. A Harvard research study deems, "maintaining meaningful relationships may play an important role in health, happiness, and longevity." And there's another bonus: 'Good, close relationships appear to buffer us from the problems of getting old," says Dr. Robert Waldinger, a psychiatrist with Harvard-affiliated Massachusetts General Hospital.[2] Those older men in Munich and the crusty cabbies in Dublin intuitively get that. It's quite simple, really: want to add years to your lifespan? Invest in gracious friendships! They may well be the elusive elixir of youth for which we gals are always searching!

Souls Knit Together

Is there a more beautiful story of friendship than that of Jonathan and David? Their bond was instantaneous and unswerving: "Now it came about when he had finished speaking to Saul, that the soul of Jonathan was knit to the soul of David, and Jonathan loved him as himself." (1 Samuel 18:1).

Souls knit together. That wording perfectly describes gracious friendship, so let's look a bit closer and discover what we gals can learn from two brawny guys who had unswerving gracious friendship down pat.

Jonathan, the son of Israel's King Saul, began his friendship with David on the battlefield when David dropped a big lug named Goliath with a little rock. We can only guess at the psychology behind this relationship. Perhaps Jonathan needed someone to champion because his father lacked a noble heart. Maybe David needed a man who believed in him after growing up marginalized by his older brothers.

The two men made a covenant right then and there, and Jonathan became the peacemaker between his father and David. In an authoritarian culture, where sons would serve their fathers to their dying breaths, Jonathan instead chose loyalty to his friend David, which was a gutsy move.

To say Saul was ticked off is a gross understatement. Saul furiously roared at Jonathan: "You son of a perverse, rebellious woman! … As long as David lives on the earth, neither you nor your kingdom will be established" (1 Sam. 20:30a, 31a). Yikes! That was signed, sealed, and delivered rage. I wouldn't be surprised if Saul threw things at Jonathan during that rant.

But Jonathan didn't cower or change his mind; he had long settled the loss of his kingdom. The day he met David, Jonathan put his royal robe on David's shoulders and gave him his sword, bow, and belt. Jonathan saw a friend he wholeheartedly believed in. Later, when David was running for his life from King Saul, he and Jonathan swore, "The Lord will be between me and you, and between my descendants and your descendants forever" (1 Sam. 20:42).

King Saul and Jonathan died in battle. And even though Saul had relentlessly hunted David for years to kill him, David mourned his death and honored him as king. Soon afterward, David became king of Israel and reigned forty years. Traditionally, a newly crowned king executed all of the descendants of a former ruler, but David sought out the relatives of Jonathan's to honor them. He found one, a disabled boy named Mephibosheth. David then protected and provided for Mephibosheth his entire life. David's loyalty to Jonathan and his descendants was unswerving and lifegiving (1 Samuel 18—2 Samuel 9).

Life-giving Truths About Gracious Friendships

The relationship between Jonathan and David paints a price-less portrait of authentic friendship that can teach us modern-day gals life-giving truths. One of those truths is straightforward: heart-commitment friendship changes lives.

Where I live, we joke that a good friend won't even take you to the hospital if it's out of her way. When my kids were in preschool, one of my friends had a child with serious health problems. She was hurt when other moms would not inconvenience their scheduled nap or story times to include her special-needs son in their activities. Those women had no bandwidth for commitment outside of their rigid schedules.

Observing this, I decided that my response to this mom would always be a *yes*. She was not a demanding person, and I knew she had a tough life ahead. If she needed a favor or wanted to get our kids together, my answer was yes. I once heard self-help guru Tim Ferriss quote the decision-making adage, "If you can't say, 'Aw, hell yes!' then it's a '*no*.'"[3] For me, my commitment to my friend was, "*Aw, hell yes! The kids can get back to their regularly scheduled naps tomorrow!*"

In Jonathan and David's story, their commitment to each another carried them through life-or-death situations. Those two men said, "*Aw, hell yes!*" time and time again!

Where friendships are concerned, most of us are not facing life-or-death issues. More often than not, we deal with matters of wounded pride and unforgiveness. The slightest offense derails many friendships today. And we often invest more energy and time in our social media followers than the people we rub shoulders with daily.

Gracious friends walk on higher ground. They assume the best about others and champion them. They invest time and energy in relationships. They choose forgiveness when things go amuck. Commitment—come hell or high water—distinguishes a gracious friendship.

Another truth is that we build honor through how we talk to and about our friends. Jonathan answered his father's accusations about David with honor for his friend. He didn't allow lies about David to stand uncontested.

> *"Then Jonathan spoke well of David to Saul his father and said to him, 'Do not let the king sin against his servant David, since he has not sinned against you, and since his deeds have been very beneficial to you. For he took his life in his hand and struck the Philistine, and the Lord brought about a great deliverance for all Israel; you saw it and rejoiced.'"* (1 Sam. 19:4-5)

Jonathan honored David and defended him to King Saul—even at risk of great personal expense. Don't we all long for a friend like that?

A gracious friend actively builds honor for her friends among other people. I learned this several years ago from Dennis Bontrager, a young youth minister. Whenever he told me about others, he described all kinds of wonderful things about them. By the time we met, I already loved them! He created an environment where his friends honored one another even before meeting.

If you're a parent, you may see this principle in action when you meet the friends of your children. I could always tell by our first interactions whether my kid had built me up as an amazing mom or tore me down with complaints and criticism.

Dennis Bontrager modeled exceptionally gracious friendship even after he lost his staff position. This young man, only twenty-one at the time, carried our church family with godly leadership while we searched for a lead pastor. When our church hired someone, Dennis gave us a farewell with only a 24-hour notice. He spoke about nothing except praise to God for our church and tremendous hope for its future. In the following days, weeks, and now, years since, Dennis has never spoken poorly about how the church treated him.

It's a life-changer when you see a young man in his twenties living with greater maturity and grace than you possess. Dennis taught me that when I speak poorly about those who have hurt or disappointed me, I'm only building dishonor for myself. A gracious friend talks long and loud about the great things she sees in her friends and keeps tightlipped about the dirt.

A deep, abiding, gracious friendship sometimes means giving up your rights. Now stay with me here because I can hear you sputtering. I'm a total proponent of boundaries; I'm not advocating a doormat mentality. We should have clarity about what is and isn't okay in any relationship. However, a good friend sometimes lays down her rights in the relationship so that the best can come forth. I can have every right to be hurt or frustrated in a friendship, but if I choose to hold on to that right, it may end up wounding not only that friendship but others. Instead, I can surrender my right to be hurt to God and let Him carry it. Then, I'm free to explore with that friend the circumstances of that hurt.

I really dorked up a few years ago with my best friend, Joanne. She told me something personal, and I shared it with one of our mutual friends. I'm less private than Joanne, and I honestly forgot that what she told me was for my ears only. Joanne had every right to be hurt and offended. She had every right to no longer trust me as a good friend and take steps to distance herself. Luckily for me, Joanne didn't hold on to those rights. She chose to forgive me and trust that I was committed to her as a true friend. With no anger, accusation, or distrust, she simply asked me about my blunder. I felt loved, valued, and trusted—even though I had messed up! Joanne's gracious approach created a deeper vulnerability and repentance in me because she didn't lash at me with her hurt and disappointment.

The New Testament tells us, "Love does not act unbecomingly; it does not seek its own, is not provoked, does not take into account a wrong suffered, does not rejoice in unrighteousness, but rejoices with the truth; bears all things, believes all things, hopes all things, endures all things (1 Corinthians 13:5b-7). I've often meditated on the phrasing "does not take into account," which means *not just letting things go but not putting them in an account at all!* The cultural belief that we're to always act in our best interest is insidious. The ideas of sacrifice and deference are no longer admirable but suspect.

In the often-understated nature of Scripture, we read that on the day Jonathan and David met, "Jonathan stripped himself of the robe that was on him and gave it to David, with his armor, including his sword and his bow and his belt" (1 Samuel 18:4). Those were highly personal items, specially fitted to Jonathan, and they carried all of his authority as a son of King Saul. In that moment, did Jonathan feel defenseless? I don't think so. Instead, I believe Jonathan felt secure and whole. He graciously valued friendship with David above his own reputation and rested in that perspective. Wow!

Friendship Misconceptions

Some misconceptions definitely deter friendships. One such belief grips many college-age folks today. A few years ago, I had a college-age gal over for dinner. She is a smart student, a thoughtful Christian, and a delightful friend. Our conversation was broad, varied, and invigorating. But when politics came up, she said, "I could never be friends with someone who believes there should be a wall."

I burst out laughing. "That's bull," I said. "Look at Supreme Court Justices Ruth Bader Ginsberg and Antonin Scalia! They couldn't have been farther apart in their political views, and yet they were lifelong friends who enjoyed family vacations together. You couldn't be friends with someone with a different view on how to run the country? Do you realize how narrow-minded and petty that view is?"

We both ended that evening with plenty of food for thought and a deeper understanding of not just our views on immigration, but also friendship and commitment.

Sadly, a rigid mindset characterizes many college students these days: "If we don't agree, we can't be friends." There's no curiosity about the other person: Why do you think that? How long have you held that belief? Do you have a reasonable argument for your belief? How important is the opinion to your overall daily life? Their entire existence has been reduced to a one-dimensional concept: are you for a wall or against a wall? In my years at Stanford, it is only recently that I've heard every variant of this theme: I could never be friends with…someone who voted for Trump; someone who says Blue lives matter; someone who doesn't ask for my pronoun, someone who is a Republican, someone who is a Democrat, and so on. I shake my head in wonder and think, Well, enjoy your pintsized life with your little circle of like-minded friends! Goodbye diversity and openness, adios free speech and curiosity.

You don't have to agree on everything to be friends with someone. Open minds and hearts are gamechangers where gracious friendship is concerned. Allow gracious multi-dimensional thinking the opportunity to expand and deepen your circle of friends. You'll find a wealth of knowledge and friendship when you open your mind and heart!

Misconceptions about time are also toxic to nurturing gracious friendships. The woman who says she doesn't have time for friendships is right; without close friendships she won't have time because she will likely live as someone committed to maximum solo productivity and ultimate convenience. Do we value efficiency that much? Is inconvenience so repugnant? Does personal independence deserve such safeguarding?

Let me illustrate through this visual given to incoming freshman at Stanford. I take a large clear jar, and I have three big rocks sitting next to it, along with lots of medium size rocks and some sand. I first pour in the sand, which represents the little chores, commitments, and extra activities available on campus. Next, I add the medium rocks, signifying essential activities. At this point, usually only one big rock will fit in the jar, and it symbolizes their most important priorities (with the other one or two big rocks left out). Then, I pour everything out and begin again. This time, I first insert the three large rocks, the medium stones second, and fill in with all the remaining sand. And it all fits! It is shortsighted to say you don't have time for significant, life-giving relationships.

Availability is a gift we can offer our friends. Especially in our hurried and competitive atmosphere, a gracious woman who makes herself available to others will attract beautiful friends to herself like a magnet. She is the one who offers help on homework, gives you a ride to the car shop, and brings meals when your entire family is sick. She offers kindness, compassion, and a listening ear. A gracious friend has an amazing capacity to see beyond her schedule and limitations and genuinely care for another human being. She makes time for a beach trip, a picnic, and a fun night out. In the process, she will be the one with deeper satisfaction in life.

Last but far from least, living for self freezes friendships. The mindset *I'm happier on my own; I need to take care of me and focus on my path* leads to an empty and arid life. It's in relationships—however messy, awkward, or inconvenient—that we fully understand ourselves and cherish our existence. We honor God when we embrace the truth that every individual we meet has value. There may be things we don't agree with or particularly enjoy about someone, but God designed every human being you and I meet for significance and purpose. It takes a gracious person to see that value, honor it, and nurture it to fruition, just as Jonathan and David did.

My friend, Floyd Thompkins of San Francisco Theological Seminary, puts it this way: "Just because someone refuses to see you does not mean you are invisible. It means the immensity of your beauty far exceeds their imagination about God's creation."

Make sure you open your eyes and heart to the beauty of others. A gracious friend is a gift like no other. When you are that friend, you not only color the world with hope and joy, but you also become an even more beautiful you.

Meaningful Dialogue

1. Do you have a friend with whom you share a deep commitment and relationship? How did you get there?

2. How have you exercised forgiveness in your friendships? Is there anyone you need to be reconciled with now?

3. Are you envious of the friendship described between Jonathan and David, or is loyalty a strong characteristic in your friends?

4. What are ways your friendships could grow in closeness, honor, and commitment?

Declarations for Gracious Living

I am a friend who sticks closer than a brother. (Proverbs 18:24)

I am rooted and grounded in love; therefore, I can give and receive love from my friends. (Ephesians 3:17)

Whatever is true, honorable, pure, and lovely, I dwell on these things, and they are being reproduced in my life. (Philippians 4:8)

4

Living in the Love Lab

"My beloved is mine, and I am his."
SONG OF SOLOMON 2:16A

In spite of the mountains of Legos® and laundry spilling out of their little house, Dan and Tracy, the parents of four energetic kids, embody a refreshingly gracious marriage. They dig each other. I mean this couple competes at honoring each other!

Tracy grew up with two brothers; Dan was surrounded by sisters. He wants any constructive criticism coming his way sandwiched between two positive comments, but Tracy's communication is direct and swift. They've invested the time to flesh out these little nuances because they assume the best about each other. Dan and Tracy continually search for ways to demonstrate thoughtfulness.

When I applauded Tracy's marriage, she just laughed and said, "I really like who Dan is. We learn from each other; he's always trying to grow and improve. And he's such a goofball. I love that about him."

Dan views their marriage as a safe haven where all the good feelings reside. "Whenever Tracy and I have a disagreement, I want to work through it and get back to our normal, which is feeling pretty good together. We don't wallow in it or get hung up on problems. We work through it and then let it go." Dan and Tracy are delightful to be around. They also inspire my hopefulness for godly marriages in the next generation.

The Book of Nehemiah is also a goldmine for inspiration and insights, echoing much of what is inside marriage books. It's an action-packed story about building amidst difficulty, distraction, and opposition. Sounds like marriage—building a beautiful family culture against all the odds. Read Nehemiah for yourself and check out the following parallels that will fill any marriage with graciousness.

Genuine Concern and Inquiry Establish the Tone

The Book of Nehemiah is dated around 823 BC. It begins with an inquiry about Jerusalem and Jewish survivors from the Babylonian captivity. When the prophet Nehemiah discovered Jerusalem's walls were in shambles and his compatriots were distressed, he said, "I sat down and wept and mourned for days; and was fasting and praying before the God of heaven" (Neh. 1:4) This smart guy was not afraid to ask the hard questions. He suspected the answers might be negative, but he truly wanted to know.

Likewise, inquiry and genuine concern mark a good marriage. It's not a gracious relational stance to whistle in the dark, feigning ignorance of hard feelings or tough circumstances.

Are you curious about your spouse? Do you know his dreams and struggles? Such abiding interest is a trait I admire in Dan and Tracy's relationship. While other marriages may slide into ambivalence or independent living, they maintain an enduring attentiveness toward each other. When Tracy showed signs of burnout from raising four young children, Dan sprang into action. As her husband, he cared about Tracy's well-being and asked the crucial questions to understand her situation.

It's so easy to fall into the trap of neglecting your spouse! John Gottman's bestseller, *The Seven Principles for Making Marriage Work,* is a terrific read for those wanting to graciously embody marriage. Gottman and his colleagues performed exhaustive observation and analysis of married couples. The results of that research shaped Gottman's "Seven Principles."

Gottman states, "At the heart of the Seven Principles approach is the simple truth that happy marriages are based on a deep friendship. By this I mean a mutual respect for and enjoyment of each other's company. These couples tend to know each other intimately—they are well versed in each other's likes, dislikes, personality quirks, hopes, and dreams. They have an abiding regard for each other and express this fondness not just in the big ways but through small gestures day in and day out."[4]

Gottman's "love lab" revealed the same genuine curiosity and concern modeled by the ancient story of Nehemiah: ask the hard questions; although the answer may be difficult to hear, genuine interest brings healing.

Prayer and Humility Define Gracious Marriage

Nehemiah prayed to God thirteen times for help. He prayed a long prayer when he learned of Jerusalem's destruction. When he stood before the king, the prophet breathed what appears to be a five-second prayer (2:4). He also prayed when he encountered opposition (4:9) and when he recounted the sacrifices he made (5:19). Nehemiah prayed when he was attacked (6:9, 14). And the Book of Nehemiah ends with this prayerful sentence: "Remember me, O my God, for good" (13:31).

Nehemiah demonstrated the power of prayer to change a situation. Could the same be said of your marriage? Do you pray alone and with your spouse when you encounter difficulty? Before important meetings? When you recount the good you've done or the help you need? It requires humility to say, *God, I don't know what to do, but You do.* What a healing balm you can offer your spouse to simply pray for him in times of difficulty or uncertainty! Prayer doesn't occur in a vacuum. We encounter a living God through our prayers—and mountains move.

One day, God gave my friend, Joanne, a picture of her marriage. In it, a beautiful light shimmered gold as her husband, Ben, lifted her into the arms of God. She said, "The way Ben loves me sets me free to be who I'm created to be."

When you and I pray for our spouses, whether it's a lengthy discourse or just a quick, silent prayer, we lift them into the arms of God.

Gracious Marriages Steady Themselves

We all face a daily barrage of stress and joy-sucking activities. Owning a thoughtful response to difficulty smooths a bumpy road into a tolerable trek. Not only did Nehemiah pray in times of attack, but he also encouraged folks to stay the course (4:14), fight distraction (6:3), and patrol the boundaries (13:5,10). With threats surrounding them, Nehemiah urged people to work with one hand and hold a sword in the other.

Dan relates to that protective posture. "In Silicon Valley, everything is more significant than your marriage," he explains. "There's not much external positive reinforcement that my marriage matters." Dan and Tracy work diligently to protect their bond in a multitude of ways. Such protection includes guarding against online addictions and relationships with other men and women. It also includes ensuring they have enough dedicated time together and prioritizing life-giving activities. Even protecting the family calendar from spinning out of control can be a gracious act.

Genesis 2:24 states, "For this reason a man shall leave his father and his mother and be joined to his wife; and they shall become one flesh." Many couples recoil from this definition of leaving their parents to cling to their spouse. Consequently, priorities get muddled, and as Gottman explains, the muddle often lands between the wife and mother-in-law. He writes:

> *"At the core of the tension is a turf battle between the two women for the husband's love. The wife is watching to see whether her husband backs her or his mother. She is wondering, 'Which family are you really in?' …The only way out of this dilemma is for the husband to side with his wife against his mother.*
>
> *Although this may sound harsh, remember that one of the basic tasks of marriage is to establish a sense of 'we-ness' between husband and wife. So, the husband must let his mother know that his wife does indeed come first."*[5]

Whether facing struggles within or threats from the outside, gracious couples discover the steadying secret to fending off attacks and maintaining a strong core.

Strategic Planning Is Everything

Nehemiah achieved in fifty-two days what had not been done in many long years. His prayerful and strategic planning focused on his goal, and he accomplished it.

Do you and your mate grasp the goal for your marriage? At the start of his story, Nehemiah stated his goal clearly in his prayer:

> *"Remember the word which You commanded Your servant Moses, saying, 'If you are unfaithful I will scatter you among the peoples; but if you return to Me and keep My commandments and do them, though those of you who have been scattered were in the most remote part of the heavens, I will gather them from there and will bring them to the place where I have chosen to cause My name to dwell"* (Neh. 1:8-9).

Nehemiah worked strategically to ensure Israel was gathered safely into Jerusalem. He said, "We are going to follow You, O God. Now gather us together as a nation and protect us!" This purpose and conviction sustained Nehemiah past every conflict, every obstacle, and into the destiny he knew was theirs.

Understanding the purpose of your marriage will lift you above the stress and distraction impeding your path. Diligently enacting a plan that leads to your goal will bring success. I witness this thoughtful planning in Dan and Tracy's family. They understand the family culture they desire, and plan their calendar accordingly. They don't get overbooked and run their family into the ground. Dan and Tracy value a close sense of community, so their life plan maps to that goal. It honors deeply satisfying friendships over a thin layer of acquaintances.

Inspect your marriage goals and pinpoint key actions that prove strategic. You will accomplish a gracious family culture that influences generations to come.

Add These Gracious Habits

When gracious living is absent in a marriage, we cringe. And we are awed when graciousness shines in a couple. However, as almost every married couple can attest, marriage seems to be the most challenging relationship to express graciousness. Beyond the four observations from Nehemiah, here are four habits that can help you solidify your marriage and nurture graciousness toward each other.

• **Watch your mouth.** Not every season of marriage is springtime and butterflies. Highs and lows exist, and life's pressures are relentless. A safe haven can swirl into a murky swamp when you mix in children, multiple careers, bills, and health issues. So, set some gracious behavior ground rules, beginning with how you speak. You see, your words reveal the health of your relationship. A happy couple will brag on each other and speak with affection. Their words will be marked by sweet contentment. Struggling couples can't stop talking in bitter tones. Their minds are filled with accusation and their speech with contempt.

Whenever grace and compassion have exited my own conversations, and I'm stewing in accusation and criticism about my husband, I recognize the author. The Spirit of God in me does not dredge up every wrong thing Andy has ever done. No, Satan does. He lies and accuses to engage me in the accusation. He is deft at "accusing them before our God day and night" (Revelation 12:10).

If you find yourself lined up on the side of the accuser, stop! Ask yourself, *is this who I long to become? The relationship po-*

liceman? *The accuser and critic? No!* Release your hurt to God and proceed through forgiveness. When good feelings have been fleeting, I have whispered Psalms 19:14: "Let the words of my mouth and the meditation of my heart be acceptable in Your sight, O Lord, my rock and my Redeemer." Then, I'll enter a time of thanksgiving for all the good in my life. I purpose to turn every accusation into prayer before I share concerns, always assuming the best intentions of my husband.

Think about this: when you're biking up a hill, you don't stop pedaling because it's hard! So, don't stop moving forward in your marriage. Remain gracious and kind as you fight off those voices of accusation and criticism. Determine to focus your words less on problems and more on God's promises. By doing this, I'm learning to speak with hope about even the most daunting circumstances.

It's important to proclaim these truths out loud. Here are examples of affirmations I use in my marriage:

I have a beautiful marriage.

I love and cherish my husband. He loves and cherishes me.

I have all I need for life and godliness, and that includes my marriage.

I can handle this. Love is patient, love is kind, so I am patient and kind.

Then, when Andy and I experience failures or disappointments, I don't race into criticism. Instead, I'm thoughtful and careful, embracing the opportunity to learn, to grow, and to practice gracious living.

• **Spell love T-I-M-E.** A good friend of mine is a staff director at a large hospital. He began a program in which his nurses sit down with each new patient to discuss the hospital stay and the discharge process.

When the nurses took the time (basically an eight-minute conversation, seated and making good eye contact), the results astonished the hospital staff. Call-button activity dropped significantly. Patients did not call nurses for small grievances, such as needing more ice, a pillow shifted, and so on. The patients' anxiety levels about being hospitalized dropped because they felt seen, cared for, and heard. Nurses attended to patients thoughtfully and systematically with fewer call-button interruptions.

When my friend relayed this story, I immediately connected it to marriage relationships. If we take the time—especially during stressful moments or tough transitions—to sit down with our spouses, make eye contact, and listen to what concerns them, the anxiety levels will plummet in our homes.

Maybe you don't currently sense a level of anxiety in your marriage, but irritation, criticism, and distancing all stem from not feeling cared for, seen, or heard. This reality is why I'm a fan of date nights. When Andy and I schedule a time each week to have fun, relax, talk, and plan, we experience greater satisfaction in our marriage. What we do on a date night is irrelevant compared to the intention behind it. The goal is to enjoy time together and understand each other—to bond and nurture our sense of "we-ness."

Gottman's research followed up on couples who attended his marriage workshop. He discovered that successful marriages stayed on track by utilizing a weekly date night and an additional hour each week described as a "state of the union meeting." In that one hour, couples talk about the highs and lows of their relationship that week. Gottman suggests ending the time with each spouse asking and answering the question: "What can I do to make you feel loved this coming week?" This regular time investment creates a gracious marriage climate.

• **Understand your purpose.** Recently, I joined a group of professionals designing an international conference. We detailed the event for months, agonizing over every decision. Then, a cloud seemed to descend on us, and I suddenly felt confused as to the actual purpose of the conference. To my surprise, when I asked what our overall goal was, I got crickets. No one remembered why we were doing the event or what we hoped to accomplish! We had forgotten the *why*!

You may laugh and say this is your work environment every day, but sadly, many marriages forget the *why* as well. Why are you married? Why are you married to this particular person? What are your goals, and what do you hope to accomplish? Do you remember? Does your spouse? Many of us have forgotten the purpose of our marriage. Is it to bring happiness and personal fulfillment? Birth children? Represent Christ to a watching world? Is it to merely survive the test of time? What is the why behind your marriage?

Let me pose a theoretical question. What's better: a restful spa retreat or an action-packed Disneyland vacation? The answer? Well, it depends on what you want to accomplish! If you are seeking a mindful vision-casting time, the spa retreat is probably prime. But what if you hope to infuse your family time with fun and high energy? In this case, the Disney vacation would be more suitable. The *why* behind your *what* matters.

By the world's standards, marriage is a 50/50, mutually beneficial relationship, vying for the most satisfying outcomes for both husband and wife. And don't get me wrong, we all deserve these outcomes. If I understand the biblical definition of marriage correctly, however, Christians are called to an entirely different relationship. Beyond the beneficial aspects, a Christian marriage symbolizes the relationship between Christ and the church. In Ephesians 5, the Apostle Paul carefully spelled out the deeper meaning of marriage. He said, "Husbands, love your wives, just as Christ also loved the church and gave Himself up for her" (5:25). Marriage is then a prophetic representation of how Christ sacrificed for the church.

Paul continued, "So husbands ought also to love their own wives as their own bodies. He who loves his own wife loves himself; for no one ever hated his own flesh, but nourishes and cherishes it, just as Christ also does the church" (5:28-29). This biblical relationship soars high above the mutually beneficial model of the world. (Mind you, it was also written during a time when women enjoyed few rights!) Husbands are called to nurture and cherish their wives as they would take care of their own bodies, in the sacrificial way that Christ loved His church.

Paul concluded his instruction on marriage with this: "Nevertheless, each individual among you also is to love his own wife even as himself; and the wife must see to it that she respects her husband" (5:33). The obligation to love and respect remains a visible testament to a godly and gracious Christian marriage.

Better Together

In Silicon Valley, people often talk about *synergy*. The word is in the title of everything from software to chiropractic offices to education. But what exactly does it mean? *Synergy* describes the cooperation between two agents to produce a combined effect more significant than the sum of their separate parts. When Andy and I got hitched in 1991, we believed we were better together than apart. We believed in the synergy of our relationship; our marriage would generate greater good than either of us could alone.

After twenty-eight years with this guy, I agree even more strongly in this principle. Jointly, we are better decision-makers. We more attentively listen to others, and our counsel to friends is rounded and complete. We correct each other's misperceptions and complete each other's goals. Together, we certainly enjoy life more than we would alone.

Ecclesiastes sums this up:

> *"Two are better than one because they have a good return for their labor. For if either of them falls, the one will lift up his companion. But woe to the one who falls where there is not another to lift him up. Furthermore, if two lie down together they keep warm, but how can one be warm alone. And if one can overpower him who is alone, two can resist him. A cord of three strands is not quickly torn apart."* (4:9-12).

If your marriage wears thin, remember that two are better than one, and a cord of three strands (you, your spouse, and Almighty God) holds strong. Together, you will accomplish greater things than you would alone. Your perspective expands from the "me" to "we." When you love each other well, you present a real-life picture of Jesus loving the church. He nurtured and cherished believers, and marriage somehow reminds the watching world what real love looks like. Instead of striving after a mutually beneficial arrangement, we are seeking a mutually serving and giving relationship. And let me be the first to tell you, it isn't natural to possess that kind of marriage; it's supernatural! It's a God-infused relationship of two people committed to honoring each other's good. It's graciousness in action every day.

Meaningful Dialogue

1. How are you pursuing a friendship with your spouse?

2. Where do you struggle to be gracious in your marriage?

3. Do any areas of your life need better boundaries to ensure a stronger marriage?

4. Do you have regular date nights and "state of the union" meetings? How about regular prayer times together? Share how these experiences strengthen your marriage bond.

Declarations for Gracious Living

I am my beloved's, and he is mine. (Song of Solomon 6:3)

I rejoice in hope for my marriage. (Romans 12:12)

I persevere through every trial in my marriage. (Romans 12:12)

I am devoted to prayer for my marriage. (Romans 12:12)

My marriage is a prophetic picture of how Christ loves the church. (Ephesians 5:25)

5

Adulting with Grace

"My son, do not forget my teaching,
but let your heart keep my commandments."

PROVERBS 3:1

My daughter's voice was cracking. "Mom, I want you to know how much I appreciate you." Nicole, a college freshman, called late one night after a campus worship service. "I was in worship, Mom, thanking God for so many things. I have roomies I love and who love me. I adore my major classes, and I straight up landed in the right field of study, plus I found such a solid Christian community right away. As I was listing every goodness God has poured into my lap, I sensed the Holy Spirit say, *Nicky, your mom prayed these in.* And I just started bawling!"

Nicole and I were both crying at that point! She continued through the tears, "I realized everything that seemed to be handed to me, you labored over in prayer. You prayed I would get into this school; you prayed for my living situation, my community, and my study. And I know you have prayed that I would have the heart to recognize God's goodness in my life and receive it. I see that now. Thank you, Mom!"

That conversation will forever wrap around my heart like a warm blanket. I felt affirmed, honored, valued, and invigorated! My adult daughter had graciously recognized that my mom-prayers mattered! It was a huge deposit into my heart account. I celebrated the truth of Proverbs 10:1a: "A wise child makes a [mother] glad."

Becoming a Gracious Adult Child

Gracious adult children esteem their parents. Sure, we all understand that no one parents perfectly. Even with great resources and the best intentions, every parent misses the mark—many times! But as we mature into adults, we can focus our eyes and hearts to recognize the good in our moms and dads—and the many things they did right. Acknowledging their value and honoring them is the secret to becoming gracious adult children.

And here's the deal: Our parents crave affirmation, respect, and appreciation, especially moms. In her New York Times bestseller book, *You're Wearing That?* Deborah Tannen, wrote:

> *"Because their value as people rests largely (in the eyes of the world as well as in their own) on their success or failure as mothers, many women are troubled throughout their lives by the nagging doubt, "Did I do a good job as a mother?" These doubts can never be fully assuaged because the job entails an almost infinite number of tasks, expectations, and requirements, none of which can be performed in a way that everyone will agree is*

best. Anything a mother says or does can be held against her.[6]

We've all been there! Yet, a bit of maturity can be a game-changer. "My biggest growth since college is in my relationship with my parents," a former student, Heather, explained to me while we were catching up over coffee. She continued, "In high school, I obeyed my parents–but now my heart is so much more involved. I look back at the fierce loyalty of my tiger-mom; it was hard to bear at times, but now I appreciate how much she loves me and is committed to my good."

In the circle of life, power shifts over the years to favor the young. The parents we have looked to for love and acceptance are now looking at us, their adult children, for the same thing. So, how can we graciously and tenderly give our parents what they long to receive?

• **Offer a clean slate.** No one likes unearthing a crusty grudge harbored over decades. Do the hard work of forgiveness toward your parents. It will release you–and them–to escape shame, regret, and bitterness. Nothing helps get us out of that stuck place like forgiveness. I once filled three pages of a legal pad with everything for which I needed to forgive my dad. Line by line, I listed the offense and the impact it had on me—and line by line, I handed it to Jesus: *Lord, this is too heavy for me to carry, so I'm handing it to you. You are the just judge, not me. I release Dad to you; I release all my hurt to you, and I say that he doesn't owe me anymore.* That legal-pad list lifted a crushing weight off my chest and lightened the burden from our relationship. Grace is a clean-slate eraser.

• **Show appreciation.** Don't we all long for someone to see the good in us? You may not share your parents' political or religious views; you may not value the things they value, but you can find traits or skills you appreciate. Catch your parents doing good things and point them out! Share with them your childhood memories of their sacrifice and effort. In discussing the value of affirming mother-daughter conversations, Deborah Tannen explains:

> *"Only her daughter can give her the ultimate*
> *stamp of approval; reassurance that she did a good*
> *job as a mother. In these ways, a mother is at her*
> *grown daughter's mercy, just as her children were*
> *at hers when they were small."*[7]

Dads need affirmation too. One Christmas, after I graduated from college, I gave my dad a framed quote attributed to Mark Twain. It read:

> *"When I was a boy of fourteen, my father was so*
> *ignorant I could hardly stand to have the old man*
> *around. But when I got to be twenty-one, I was*
> *astonished at how much he had learned in seven*
> *years."*[8]

The quote was my way of apologizing to Dad for being a pill as a teenager—and expressing that I had grown to appreciate him. I realized that what I had once viewed and openly disdained as slow thinking was, in fact, deep wisdom. Almost all the areas I criticized in Dad when I was in high school turned out to be his areas of strength and wisdom.

• **Usher in peace and non-reactivity.** If you have wounds or harbor bad feelings from childhood, your parents likely do as well. Someone has to stop the cycle of reactivity in the relationship.

> *"When daughters react with annoyance or even*
> *anger at the smallest, seemingly innocent remarks,*
> *mothers get the feeling that talking to their daugh-*

*ters can be like walking on eggshells: they have to
watch every word ... The complaint I heard most
often when I talked to women about their mothers
was, 'She's always criticizing me.' The complaint I
heard most often when I talked to women about
their grown daughters was, 'I can't open my
mouth. She takes everything as criticism.'"*[9]

My daughter and I once had a terse conversation about
what she wanted for Christmas. She requested a wetsuit,
Coachella tickets, and a sound system for an upcoming gig.
While I was sputtering, "Which one?" she had to run to class.
I sent her a text that read: "Choosing one big Christmas gift;
it's a great problem to have!" But I was so impressed when
she later apologized. She calmly focused on her behavior and
graciously dispelled any hard feelings. We easily could have
slipped into a well-worn pattern of frustration. Instead, she
ushered in peace.

• **Cut the cord.** Growing up is a hard transition for everybody.
Parents don't always know when or how to stop worrying, protecting, or advising their children. As an adult child, the secret
is to give your parents less opportunity. Cut the cord! Bring
your adult self to the relationship. Respectfully communicate
something along the lines of, "Mom, Dad, I appreciate your
thoughts on this, but I've got it. I can handle this on my own."
If you want your parents to treat you as an adult, act like one.

• **Practice sensitivity to needs.** Life comes full circle when
you begin thoughtfully considering what your parents need.
Making a meal for them is a significant shift from those days
of coming home and eating all their food and drinking all the
beer! Putting gas in their car and doing little projects around
the house all clarify a beautiful reality: "I'm no longer a con-
sumer in this relationship. I care about you as a human being,

and I hold you in esteem. I'm mindful of the impact my words and actions hold in your world."

Mindful Boundaries

If your childhood brimmed with trauma and hardship, how do you relate to parents who have brought you harm? I spent years helping one student flesh out the answer to that question.

I met Sondra[10] during her freshman year at Stanford University when she made the decision to follow Christ. We met weekly to talk and study life-changing Scripture together over cups of rich, steaming coffee. One of the hardest topics she had to navigate was how to relate to her mom. A constant source of chaos and condemnation, Sondra's mother produced extreme levels of harsh judgment. Her occult beliefs and practices poisoned efforts at civil conversation; her disoriented thinking and sporadic behaviors peppered the relationship with hostility. She would unexpectedly show up at Sondra's dorm and engage in angry rants and shouting matches.

Sondra felt trapped in the toxic environment of her mother's anger and judgment. Such behavior can cripple a parent-child relationship, says Tannen. "To a daughter, a mother is larger than life, so any judgment coming from her can seem like a life sentence."[11]

For several years, Sondra refused to see her mother and would only talk to her briefly on the phone. But as Sondra grew more confident in her faith and ability to hold healthy boundaries with her mom, their relationship warmed. They cautiously ventured to see each other for short amounts of time. Their phone conversations increased. There were many steps forward and still many steps backward as they improvised their newly adult relationship. I witnessed considerable growth when Sondra could reflect on the positive traits of her mother while continuing to hold healthy boundaries. The emotions leveled off, and Sondra could progressively view her mom as she would any other adult—with both positive and negative characteristics.

Throughout this journey of navigating their relationship, I've admired Sondra's graciousness, resilience, and commitment to stay in relationship with her mother, though with mindful boundaries. Most of us don't think about whether a parent will attend a graduation ceremony. Still, for Sondra, it was a well-earned milestone to enjoy her Stanford graduation with her mother.

A word of caution: many psychologists advise against a complete disconnection with parents, unless there is physical or mental harm. However, not every parent-child relationship is salvageable. There is much work to be done with setting boundaries and understanding what is optimal for each family.

Many of us feel that our parents' behavior disqualifies them from our respect or kindness. This situation presents a conundrum. Are we responsive to the commandment to honor our father and mother, and if so, how?

Jesus, of all people, seemed to marginalize the role of parents when He called for His followers to forsake their fathers and mothers for the sake of the gospel (Matthew 4:18, 22). He said they could not be His disciples if they loved father and mother more than they loved Him. But note that in Matthew 19:18-19, Jesus cited the Fifth Commandment: "Honor your father and mother" in response to the Pharisees dodging their responsibility to provide for their parents because of religious traditions (Matt. 15:4).

The Apostle Paul confirmed that the Fifth Commandment is indeed still in place when he positioned it with his additional commentary, "Children, obey your parents in the Lord, for this is right. Honor your father and mother which is the first commandment with a promise, so that it may be well with you and that you may live long on the earth" (Ephesians 6:1-3). His next statement added a bit of weight to the other side of the relationship when he said, "Fathers, do not provoke your children to anger, but bring them up in the discipline and instruction of the Lord." So, the parent-child relationship requires effort and grace on both ends.

Honor is a boomerang. When we honor our parents, honor returns to us, and "our days are prolonged," according to Scripture. Does honor mean we put ourselves in harm's way or that we give our abusers open access to our lives? No, of course not! However, we can walk the tightrope of not speaking evil of our parents even if we don't agree with their choices. We can remain gracious, kind, and respectful, no matter what. We can keep showing up in the relationship and resist the temptation to withdraw. We may not have a good thing to say about our parents' parenting skills, but we can still honor the fact that our mother and father gave us life.

I've mentored my dear friend, Martina, since she was sixteen to now a woman in her thirties. She grew up with an absentee, alcoholic father. For years, their relationship was tenuous. She struggled with feelings of anger and disappointment toward him, but they stayed in touch. Through tremendous personal growth and forgiveness, Martina made baby steps year after year toward relationship. She learned to accept the things she couldn't change. Martina recognized her boundaries and capacity to stay connected. With eyes wide open, she honored the good in her father. As his health declined, she took responsibility for his care.

Today, Martina can honestly say that she loves her dad, and their relationship is enriching. Does she wish he had been a present and nurturing father? Sure, but that wound is no longer infected and painful. Martina's joyful testimony tells of the depth of character and grace-filled emotional maturity God brought on her behalf. Hebrews 12:11 refers to the "peaceful fruit of righteousness," which Martina owns as she cares for her dad in his last days.

The Great Inheritance

I became a Christian when I was sixteen. Both my parents were atheists. You can imagine how they responded to my newfound faith! They were embarrassed when I put a Jesus sticker on my car. But when I became more respectful, they were encouraged. I had the joy of leading my mom to Christ, and Jesus was her comfort during her last season of life.

Even while I grew as a Christian in college, the hardest place to live it out was at home with my parents. If you have a godly and peaceful heritage, thank the Lord for that inheritance! If home is a tough place, I want to encourage you to do two things.

First, look to Jesus for your acceptance and blessing. It may be that your parents don't have blessings to give. Dig into the Lord, and you will experience the love, forgiveness, and acceptance for which your heart longs. You don't need to walk this world as an orphan when your Heavenly Father wants to hold you near.

Second, remind yourself daily that honor is a boomerang. No matter how poorly your parents may act, you can choose to honor them with respect and appreciation. The Apostle Paul wrote instructions to slaves on how to respond to their masters: "Whatever you do, do your work heartily, as for the

Lord rather than for men, knowing that from the Lord you will receive the reward of the inheritance. It is the Lord Christ whom you serve" (Colossians 3:23-24).

You have within you the capacity to love and honor because you are doing it for God. He promises an inheritance to you as a reward. And that inheritance is the greatest gift a gracious adult child can ever receive.

Meaningful Dialogue

1. What do you appreciate about your upbringing? What are the ways you can express your affection and gratitude toward your parents?

2. When do you need God's strength in your relationship with your parents?

3. How do you communicate healthy boundaries with your parents? Is this difficult?

4. Where does there need to be healing and forgiveness in your relationship with your parents?

5. Is honor a part of your family culture? If not, how could you incorporate it into your relationship?

Declarations for Gracious Living

I bless my mother and father in Jesus' name! (Matthew 19:19)

God knew me before I was in the womb. (Psalm 139)

He has set me apart and appointed me to this life. (Jeremiah 1:5)

My inheritance is beautiful. (Psalm 16:6)

6

The Value of Children

*"Hear, my son, your father's instruction
and do not forsake your mother's teaching."*

PROVERBS 1:8

It was the summer of 2004, and I had joined a neighborhood swimming pool with a few mom friends. The pool couldn't have been uglier—thirty feet of rectangular mottled-gray concrete surrounded by a rusty chain-link fence. Yet, the price was right, so we sucked our mommy tummies into our suits, slathered on sunscreen, and jumped in!

Eager to get in thirty minutes of girl talk, we quickly conspired to corral our kids for group swimming lessons. The kids sat in ankle-deep water on the pool steps with their teacher while we moms were happily chatting—until Diane's daughter padded up to her in tears. She was a bit cautious in new situations and was not at all on board with the swim lessons. Gone was our thirty-minute respite. The money for those lessons was dogpaddling away with every minute Diane's little girl re-fused to stick a tiny toe into the pool.

Dare I tell you what I would've done if the reticent four-year-old had been my kid? Embarrassed and frustrated, I probably would have hissed in her ear, "You had better get your little mermaid ass into that pool or else!"

Yep, I had a lot of growing to do back then! But not my friend Diane. In the twenty years I've known her, I've never heard her raise her voice or treat her children harshly. Instead, she hugged her trembling daughter, calmly asked some questions, and told her she could stay with us for five minutes, and then she had to at least sit on the steps with her feet in the pool. By the middle of the second lesson, her little girl had transitioned from tentatively sitting on the steps to full-splash participation.

If Diane was frustrated, she never displayed it. And let me note here, if a parent shows dishonor and disrespect for a child, other people will follow suit. None of the other moms or kids even noticed the problem because of the grace and patience Diane modeled.

Value Your Children

Gracious parenting is a seed watered by emotional maturi-ty—one that bears fruit for generations. These days, I'm liv-ing in the harvest season of parenting, and I can attest that all the hard days and sleepless nights were worth the effort! Squabbles and tears have faded into the past, along with the monotony of never-ending snacks, meals, treats, and dishes. The Legos® have long been boxed up, and although I don't miss the exhaustion of parenting small children, I certainly miss the tenderness of those days. What I'm beginning to em-brace with my children, who are mostly running on their own these days, are gratifying adult relationships. Much of the fruit of my labor extends before my eyes.

Reflecting on what I would do differently raising my children, my mind races past every stressor that road-bumped my early parenting days, stressors that I now see were irrelevant: keeping my home neat, caring what other people thought of my kids or me, doing well at work and being perceived as doing well, and on and on. My mind blows past all of those things and locks on a memory of my daughter: she is young and upset about something. In a momentary exchange, all I can see is her asking, in one way or another, *"Mom, am I important? Am I worthy of love, honor, and attention? Am I delightful? Am I enough? Mom, do you like me?"* When I look back at parenting, my child's uplifted, questioning face is all I can see, and the truth is crystal clear: In many moments that appear trivial, our children are learning if they are valuable and cherished—or not.

I can recall the times I was genuinely valued as a child and the impact those moments had on me. I remember the first time my Uncle Lou drove to Texas from California with his new wife, Beth. She was twenty years younger than him, blonde and braless. They were both psychologists. Everything about them was fascinating and unlike my orderly, middle-class upbringing. They arrived for a two-week stay with all their clothes stashed in brown-paper grocery bags. They took showers together, played tennis, and enjoyed long walks with me. We talked, and my opinions and feelings seemed to matter.

Receiving respect and approval from my cool uncle was like oxygen to my young heart, so I decided I wanted to become a psychologist. I read all of Freud's writings in fourth grade, and I would write back-and-forth letters with my Aunt Beth and Uncle Lou, discussing various theories. How I would love to read one of those letters now!

When I reflect on that first vacation with Uncle Lou and Aunt Beth, a crystal-clear snapshot appears: they gazed square-on at me. No distractions about the house or laundry or meals or work or other people butted me out of their line of vision. They were fully present, which communicated to me that I mattered. I was worthy of their time and attention. And not only that, they delighted in me. They genuinely valued me as a human being!

Sometimes, I wonder if parenting boils down to feelings. *Does the child feel cherished? Liked? Important? Powerful? How about that little girl who was frightened about swim lessons? Did she feel important and loved, even though she was disrupting the mommy-time plan?*

What if gracious parenting boils down from soccer games, the endless driving to activities, the tedium of laundry and meals and planning (where we as parents spend most of our time), into something as basic as a feeling? *Did my parents enjoy me and cherish me as a person? Did they see me for who I was, not who I could become? Did they dig me? Or was I a chore? An embarrassment? Another mouth to feed? An obstacle to their own fun and personal leisure?*

I once watched an interview with Oprah, who said all the guests of her show shared one commonality—everyone she interviewed, royalty and rock star alike, asked at the end, "Was that ok? Did I do ok?" She concluded that we all are asking that question. We, as parents, have the privilege and responsibility of graciously answering that question for our precious children.

The Grace of Faith

Beyond our children's relationship with us, we have the honor of establishing their bond with Jesus Christ. I know many parents who make three common missteps here. One, they say, "I don't want to force religion on my children; they can decide for themselves when they are older." Ironically, these parents aren't following the same logic with music or sports or academics. No one says, "I'll let my children decide as adults if they want to play soccer." Parents know that such timing will be too late!

Two, they don't present spiritual grounding in a thoughtful way. We discovered this mistake when our eight-year-old said, "I don't know if I believe that Jesus is the only way to God. What about my friends who are Buddhist or Hindu?" I remember staring at her wide-eyed and thinking, *Uh-oh!* We had always discussed Jesus in a childlike way, but our daughter craved more in-depth information. We quickly switched to offering more apologetics to help her make sense of her multicultural world, and we moved toward experiential learning.

The adage, A person with an experience is never at the mercy of a person with an argument, stands true. I knew our children would encounter the intense debates of college professors, but I made sure they experienced the love of God and His speaking voice in their lives. There is no junior Holy Spirit! The Holy Spirit fills children, as well as adults.

The third misstep we parents make is not representing Christ well in our homes. We all have thoughtless, hypocritical, unredeemed ways that impede our children's embrace of Jesus as Lord and Savior. When our sin distorts a child's picture of Jesus (or a godly mom), we need to be transparent and honest about it. Many times, I had to hold one of my children in my arms, look them in the eye and say, "Mommy was wrong to say that. A godly mom doesn't act that way, and I'm sorry I let my anger come out. Will you forgive me?"

A good friend of mine realized she had often let fear control her decisions. She had modeled for her children a form of Christianity that partnered with fear and dread more than faith and trust. Because she valued her children knowing Christ in compelling ways, she asked her children to tell her whenever they heard her partnering with fear. My friend's newly transparent walk with God enabled her children to shun fear and embrace the warmth of faith and trust.

Let your children see your walk with God! They should encounter you studying the Word, kneeling in prayer, hear you singing praise to God as part of normal life. Most of all, we parents must be the emissaries of the love of God to our children—their first vision of His light and love. And that's a sobering responsibility. Our children capture the vision and purpose for their lives through our words and actions.

I often think of God's words to Jeremiah, "Before I formed you in the womb, I knew you, and before you were born, I consecrated you; I have appointed you..." (Jer. 1:5). These words remind me that God has a plan for each of us. As parents, we are called to search out and affirm the destiny God has placed on each child's life. What a precious honor and responsibility!

Ages and Stages

When children are young, that's the time to put on graciousness and gentleness like a favorite sweater—get comfortable with it and wear it often! Gracious parenting at this phase creates gracious children. Research backs me up when I tell you that rude, impatient parenting creates rude, irritable children. All that yelling or nagging cuts children off from their empathy skills. They will emulate what they have experienced at home.

Some kids in the preschool years love small motor activities, such as coloring and painting. Others can't sit for five minutes without running outside to jump on tricycles. Comparison often rears its ugly head, and parents agonize over a child not coloring well or just wanting to do one thing. Parents anxiously look for signs their child is progressing at the right pace. I knew a gracious teacher who so wisely told parents, "Everyone is working on different skills. Children grow at their own pace. Don't worry about anyone else's child; just observe and enjoy what your child is learning right now."

Gracious parenting fosters a growth mindset in your children by celebrating their efforts and hard work. This is not the season to be performance-oriented! Love warmly, be consistent, and focus on that foundation of acceptance and kindness. That's gracious parenting!

When my kids moved into those bumpy teenage years, I often mused about, "Everyone is working on different skills." It steered me away from comparisons and helped me remain curious. Some kids develop socially; others are focused on sports or academics. All teens are insecure and desperately searching for their place in life. Hormones wreak havoc on their emotions while social confusion and awkwardness reign supreme.

Don't we all wince a bit when we remember our transitional teenage years? That's the cue to let your teens catch you bragging about them. You should be their biggest fan. Even when times are difficult or your relationship feels strained, release your love over them in many ways. Help them to find their place in life—what they are good at and who they are on the inside. Remind them of experiences with God that anchor their identity and purpose in Christ.

Peers in middle school and high school often ridicule and criticize each other. These experiences make for an ideal season to speak life and affirmation over your children. Find things to laugh about, and keep the good feelings flowing. Sure, it can be challenging to remain gracious in the face of rebellion and disrespect from teens. But think about it this way: When you're pulled over for speeding, the officer is usually courteous, even though you are in the act of rebellion. If he instead displays frustration or anger, all of the focus shifts to his behavior. Rather than pondering your behavior and the consequences of it, you drive away thinking, *What a jerk!* Similarly, with parenting we must graciously manage our emotions to keep our teens focused on their behavior and the consequences of it.

After children head off to college or move out of the house, our parenting should shift dramatically. If it doesn't, there will be trouble! This stage will reveal if we as parents embrace gracious and respectful behavior, even when we may not agree with lifestyle choices.

Thankfully, my children have continued to walk with God in their own vibrant faith journey. Still, there are plenty of decisions and behaviors that don't thrill me. When they've shared new political opinions or thrown words like "heteronormative" around, I pause and ask myself, *What would I say to a friend who had this opinion? Would I rant or try to convince her otherwise?* That little pause helps me respond to my kids with the same dignity and respect I would extend to a girlfriend.

As our children blossom into adulthood, budding friendship nourished by gracious and mindful actions eclipses parenting. Even at college-age and beyond, our children draw strength from our acceptance and celebration of who they are.

Wisdom for the Long Road

Wise parenting books abound, for sure. And I can't condense all aspects of gracious parenting into one chapter. However, here's some been-there wisdom for the long road of parenting.

• **Face your feelings rather than medicating.** These days, the biggest secret among moms is their reliance on alcohol. Don't fall down that slippery slope! If you drink, limit it to weekends and special occasions. I remember telling my husband on one of those long and tedious days of parenting, "You better get home before I start drinking!" I was joking, but there was some truth to my desperation around that five o'clock hour. If I had simply pressed into worshiping at Jesus' feet rather than opening that bottle of wine (or renting a movie or running out for some retail therapy), I would have been a better parent.

In the past ten years, I've seen a significant shift in the prevalence of drinking, even in church moms' groups. One young mom recently told me that whenever her women's Bible study group planned special outings, the events always involved wine. She said with chagrin, "Having a glass a wine isn't going to fill my soul." I agree. My friends, it's lawful to drink but perhaps not always profitable. Find what truly gives life and invigorates you as a parent.

• **Don't parent alone.** Solo parenting is not good for you or your child. Enlist healthy adults to join in everything from making meals together to park dates and vacations. If your mechanism of gracious self-control isn't engaged, then it helps to have folks around.

When I counsel moms struggling with anger issues, I ask, "Would you yell at your child if you had friends present?" The answer is consistently *no*. A little social accountability helps both parents and children with self-control.

Remember the simple advice of Ecclesiastes 4:9-10, "Two are better than one because they have a good return for their labor. For if one falls, the other will lift up his companion. But woe to the one who falls when there is not another to lift him up." Invest the time to build your community so your children have multiple examples of loving, gracious adults.

• **Deposit into your child's heart every day.** Look, withdrawals are inevitable. We misunderstand statements and misread signals all the time. No parent is perfectly patient, kind, and gracious 100 percent of the time. However, if you have purposed to make deposits into your child's heart every day with kind words, affirmations, time, and thoughtful experiences, occasional withdrawals are easily covered.

I find it appropriate that the Apostle Peter, known for his missteps and strong personality, said, "Above all, keep fervent in your love for one another, because love covers a multitude of sins" (1 Peter 4:8). If you have banked good feelings with your child, that love will cover a multitude of mess-ups.

• **Pray the Scriptures over your child.** The most important work of parenting is prayer. It took me forever to figure that out! So often, we speak our fear and worry or frustration to God in prayer. But don't merely pray the problem; pray the solution. If your child is being bullied or living a dangerous life, pray for deliverance from their enemies. Psalm 17:7-8 tells us, "Wondrously show Your lovingkindness O Savior of those who take refuge at Your right hand from those who rise up against them. Keep me as the apple of the eye; hide me in the shadow of Your wings." This means, *Lord, hide my child from the evil around them that they would know Your lovingkindness!*

Don't just pray, *Lord, Ella is starting to make bad choices. Please help her.* Add Psalms 90:12 to your prayer: *Lord, teach*

Ella to number her days that she may present to You a heart of wisdom.

Using Psalm 101:2, pray that your child will have personal integrity in this perverted and complicated world: "I will walk within my house in the integrity of my heart. I will set no worthless thing before my eyes."

To ensure you understand how to pray Scriptures, here's the prayer I pray for my son using Psalm 101:2, *Lord, I pray Cooper will walk within his house in the integrity of his heart. He will set no worthless thing before his eyes. Lord, this is who You made Cooper to be—a man of integrity and goodness. I bless him in Jesus' name as he turns his eye away from anything that would steal his joy or innocence.*

I pray that gratitude and worship mark my children (Psalm 103:1-5). I pray they will own prosperity and abundance with their health, work, and relationships. I ask that they fulfill God's purpose and destiny in every season of their lives. And my prayer for us as parents is pretty simple: *Lord, show us how to graciously love and lead our children just like You graciously love and lead Your people.*

The Super Tool for Gracious Parenting

One super tool will aid gracious parenting like no other. It builds margin in your schedule to vision-cast and problem solve. This tool ensures your family culture is positioned well and develops a pattern of memories and good times that graciously shape future generations. I'm talking about a sabbath.

Now before your mind races to an image of people huddled around their Bibles by candlelight, consider this: In David Allen's bestselling book *Getting Things Done,* he advocates maximum efficiency and satisfaction in work and personal life result from a weekly period of reflection.[12] No emails, no texts, or work phone calls. Use this time to step away from the details of work to evaluate the big picture, birds eye view of your life. It's a time for rest, enjoying the outdoors, perhaps reading or pursuing those back-burner interests, playing with family or pets, and reflecting. Allen, productivity consultant and executive coach, says this is the essential tool in his work with executives to gain creativity, energy, and vision for the task at hand.[13]

In our always-on, 24/7 culture, this is a hard task. When I first read Allen's book, I was exhausted and overwhelmed by the task of rearing four young children. Creativity and vision-casting for my family were far-off ideals. Shoot, I was just trying to plow through laundry and cut a path through all the toys on the floor! But Allen's tool triggered a conviction in me that I had lost sight of honoring the sabbath.

Although Allen did not use the word sabbath in his book, in my mind, he was describing the same principle. Just as a reminder, honoring the Sabbath is one of the Ten Commandments.

In Exodus 20:8 -11 God said,

> *"Remember the Sabbath day, to keep it holy. Six days you shall labor and do all your work, but the seventh day is a Sabbath of the Lord your God … For in six days the Lord made the heavens and the earth, the sea and all that is in them, and rested on the seventh day; therefore, the Lord blessed the Sabbath day and made it holy."*

If you're inclined to write off the practice of sabbath because it is linked to the Old Testament and we are no longer under the Law, I will point out that the Creation account established the model for sabbath practice. Although respecting the Sabbath is part of the Law, it has roots in Creation (before the fall of man) and therefore applies today. Jesus issued the crucial New Testament qualifier when He stated, "The Sabbath was made for man, and not man for the Sabbath" (Mark 2:27-28). Think about that: God made the Sabbath for humankind! It's a gift and a tool for living our best life! Jesus confronted the legalistic and oppressive practice of treating the Sabbath as a law because God created it as a gracious gift.

My husband and I made small changes in habits and reaped the family benefits of this gift of the Sabbath. We purposed to make Sunday a restful day. That meant the tiny changes of finishing all the laundry by Saturday, choosing not to get online or watch television, and instead having family night where we played games, worshipped, and had devotions. Andy and I used to laugh that we couldn't buy a nap on Sundays, but we sure tried.

The one big change we made—and I'm forever grateful that God led us to do this—we skip dinner on Sunday nights. Yep, you understood that right, we have breakfast before church and then a big lunch after church, and then the kitchen is closed. Why? I didn't want high-maintenance kids that wilt if you don't feed them every hour! I wanted them to develop the discipline of missing a meal once a week to gain empathy. It developed a muscle in them for mission trips where we might go a day without a real meal. In a small way, it helped them identify with the poor in the world who do not enjoy three meals each day.

It took considerable work to cordon off our Sabbath day from little league practices, playdates, work dates, homework, and more. Logically though, how could you possibly develop a healthy family culture if the family is never all together? Those were the days we not only modeled how to listen to God and enjoy His nearness, but also how to listen to each other and enjoy each other's friendship. It trained each of us to live in a mindful, restful, reflective rhythm each week. It gave us permission to pull out of frantic busyness and breathe. Embracing the grace and rest of a weekly sabbath filled us with the energy to give others grace throughout the week.

Here are my suggestions for setting aside a day for rest, reflection, and family:

- Keep the day as a gift you look forward to rather than an obligation you dread.

- Make it special! Add a fun dessert, focused circle time or worship, sharing affirmations and positive feedback, going outside, and playing together.

- Rest; don't do regular chores.

- Honor God and have specific time set aside for cultivating His friendship.

- Take time to evaluate your life and think creatively about what you want to see.

Gracious parenting is a gift you extend to your children. You are laying the foundation for their lives. You are modeling an enormity of complex decisions and relationships: how to manage their time and organize their stuff, how to relate to men, to women, to someone older and someone younger, how to resolve conflict, how to give and receive love and affection and so on. Your kindness, gentleness, and honor will nurture positive self-esteem for a great life. Better than all those music lessons and soccer games, gracious parenting is the godly, affirming, and perpetual answer to that nagging question, "Mom, am I enough?"

Meaningful Dialogue

1. What are your memories of being cherished as a child? Does this impact your parenting now?

2. When is it difficult to value and enjoy your children? How can you change your mindset in those moments?

3. How do you engage God in your parenting? Is prayer important to your relationship with your children?

4. What are the habits you need to break that are negatively impacting your family?

5. What are practical ways your family could enjoy a sabbath?

Declarations for Gracious Living

My children are a gift from the Lord! (Psalm 127:3)

I am patient. I am kind. I am not easily provoked. I can bear all things, believe all things, hope all things and endure all things because of the love of God in me. (1 Corinthians 13:4-7)

I honor the sabbath and call it a delight. (Isaiah 58:13-14)

7

Caregiving & Receiving

"The Lord will command His lovingkindness in the daytime;
And His song will be with me in the night."
PSALMS 42:8A

She was everything one would expect of an Aspen fine jeweler: whip-smart, sophisticated, and beautiful. A stylish pixie cut haloed Sharlene's salt-and-pepper hair, and thick black glasses framed Caribbean-blue eyes that reflected deep-sea soul wisdom. I liked her instantly.

While I was trying on rings, Sharlene remarked with a soft, heart-tugging sigh that chemo made her fingers too swollen to wear any of her beautiful pieces. What she said next was sheer vulnerability. "I used to have strawberry blonde hair down to my waist. This is what's grown out after the chemo; here, feel my head!" She pointed her salt-and-pepper crown toward me. I reached out to gently stroke her hair; it was velvety soft.

My fingers remembered that softness as I continued trying on rings while Sharlene talked.

"Cancer has taught me that the people standing behind you don't have knives; they have cushions. My friends have carried me through all this. Everyone says I'm the nicest person they know, and I wonder, *If I'm so good, why does all of this crap happen to me?* But I'm learning to roll with each day and be grateful."

I left Sharlene's gorgeous Aspen store with an aquamarine ring I'll always treasure, along with the memory of her velvety-soft hair and gracious spirit. After my visit, I discovered aquamarine has long been a symbol of health and hope. It's calming, soothing, and inspires truth and letting go. That's my prayer for myself and Sharlene—to graciously walk in health and hope, inspire truth, and just let go! Sure, sometimes people stab you in the back, but as Sharlene learned, most are standing beside and behind you with safety nets and cushions. Or, more practically, with soup pots, clean sheets, warm cups of herbal tea, rides to doctor appointments, babysitting, and long hugs that say, "You're not alone, my friend." These are the love language of gracious caregiving.

The Gracious Receiver

My father-in-law, the Reverend Drew Allen, died of pancreatic cancer on October 7, 2017. I'll never forget the phone call he made to us on January 19 of that year. He and my mother-in-law, Dallas, had received a doctor's report they needed to discuss with us. I pulled out my phone to record it, thinking, *Oh, I might need to remember an upcoming appointment or some meds he might need.* But we got something entirely different.

Drew quickly shot through the details of the report and told Andy and me that his life expectancy was less than a year. At length, though, he shared how he experienced God's faithfulness and provision. He bragged on God, and then he bragged on us and how proud he was of us. He prayed a blessing over us like Moses must have prayed over the children of Israel. He gave a patriarchal blessing that he would reiterate every time we visited with him until his death.

From those beautiful and rich nine months witnessing Drew's decline and being on his care team, I learned some valuable lessons about how to be a gracious receiver of caregiving.

• **Pour out your complaints to God.** For the one in need of care, receiving is not an easy place to be. We value strength, independence, and self-sufficiency. Yet many of us find ourselves as weak and dependent as a newborn. We're humbled and hurting. Maybe we're furious at our plight or wanting to blame and complain—anything to escape the prison of our broken bodies.

My father-in-law taught me to pour out complaints to God. There's no time for polite discourse or a distant nodding acquaintance with Him. Talk long and loud with God. Find real provision in His friendship and embrace the warmth of Psalm 86:7: "In the day of my trouble I shall call upon You, for You will answer me."

Even if you've not built a bank account of relationship with God, start now. He's only a prayer away. What may feel like hypocrisy or ridiculousness can grow into intimacy and real friendship. Make finding your peace with God a top priority.

• **Make peace with people.** Forgive others, not because they deserve it, but for your health. And ask others for forgiveness. Forgiveness opens avenues of health and healing. Scripture says, "If possible, so far as it depends on you, be at peace with all men" (Romans 12:18). Don't waste energy with anger. Let it go and embrace peacefulness. If you honestly don't know how, think about this key to unlocking peacefulness: "The steadfast mind You will keep in perfect peace, because he trusts in You" (Isaiah 26:3).

Focus is the key to unlocking peace. Rather than focusing on your pain or the injustice of it all, focus on God. Fix your thoughts on the love and character of Jesus Christ, and you'll discover peacefulness.

• **Give blessings.** You may wonder *How can I possibly give anyone anything? I'm weak, ill, and needy!* And yet, it's always within our power to bless others—to give caregivers patience, love, and gratitude. Those are much-needed blessings!

As my father-in-law modeled, also talk about bigger things than your calendar of doctor appointments. Talk about what people mean to you. Talk about what you learn from God. Your caregivers need to hear how you're doing and how they're doing in their care for you.

• **Communicate with your care team.** It's a kindness to keep everyone up to date, not only on your physical health but also about what you're thinking and how you're feeling about the latest stage. People will often look to you for how to interpret developments. Are you discouraged? They will understand to look for ways to be hopeful and helpful. Are you joyful in spite of difficulties? They will follow suit. Communicating graciously and thoughtfully with the people in your life brings dignity to what they are doing for you, and it dispels confusion and mystery.

• **Say TSP.** Three words go a long way in everyone's life and especially with caregivers: **Thanks, Sorry, Please.** Yes, you probably are in pain or discomfort, but it doesn't excuse you from the basic human kindnesses of saying "thank you" when help is given, "I'm sorry" when you have hurt someone, and "please" to show you are making a request and not a demand. The machinery of caregiving will run smoother with these three gracious words.

• **Consider what you can control and what to let go.** No one likes feeling out of control, and when a health crisis causes that loss, grasping at stuff to steady yourself is an understandable reaction (things like which route you take to the doctors' office, food preparation, or house cleaning). But every hill is not worth a fight. Consider what is truly important to you and then respectfully and graciously communicate wishes. On incidentals, be flexible. Don't try to backseat drive on details that are no longer your jurisdiction. People aren't going to clean your house, care for your children or pets, or do chores precisely the way you would. Don't burn out your care team because you refuse to let the small stuff slide.

• **Set folks up for success.** Put your healthcare wishes in writing. Even a twenty-year-old should have a health directive. Everyone can document in an easy-access, simple format their primary contacts, financial information, and their desired outcomes for many likely healthcare scenarios.

The first thing my father-in-law completed was a definitive health directive that outlined his wishes for many possible healthcare scenarios. He felt it wasn't fair to his wife or us to have to make those difficult and emotional decisions for him. Drew took all of the uncertainty and guilt out of decision making because he had already thoughtfully considered the choices. Multiple times he talked with us about financial information and exactly how we should ensure proper provision for his wife, Dallas. He cleaned out his hobby room so that we were not burdened with that enormous task. As much as it was possible, Drew took care of details out of honor for us.

The Sacred Privilege

When you're standing on the other side of the bed, remember this: gracious caregiving is not a chore; it's a sacred privilege. But we are afraid to draw near to it, aren't we? Our fears tumble out of us: *I don't want to impose. During such vulnerability, perhaps she prefers to be alone? Or with someone else, someone closer? What if I don't know what to do? What if it's too much for me to bear?*

Ah, the grip of *what if.* It can really hold us back. Let's pause and consider this: *If fears are tumbling out of us as caregivers, shouldn't we assume just as much fear (or more) tumbles out of someone who needs care? Is he or she not also wrestling with the vulnerability and imposition, the possible rejection—and the loneliness?*

Gracious caregiving is a sacred space filled with the raw vulnerability and needs of both the caregiver and the patient. As self-sufficient, active individuals, isn't such dependence what we want to avoid at all costs? Yet, here we are. As caregivers, do we have the courage to draw near? If we don't, who will?

Sometimes, I wonder if Facebook® has robbed us of our humanity. We hear of someone's difficulty, and we post, "So sorry." Then we add a sad-face emoji and a praying-hands emoji. And we feel done. We've checked the box for compassion and reaching out. But what we've done is check out on a sacred responsibility.

So, how can we be thoughtful and gracious caregivers? I'll list some practical ways, but first, I'll mention more about Drew's time in the hospital. Honor and care were magnified in that situation.

Some of my favorite times at the hospital with Drew were in the mornings. On my way home from dropping off carpool, I would stop by for fifteen or twenty minutes to check in with him, share what Scripture I had enjoyed that morning, and then pray together. I loved hearing his thoughts on those verses, and I think it was a welcome change for him from answering constant medical questions about his health.

I'll never forget one visit when Drew was in a shared room. The hospital chaplain came by to visit the roommate. The chaplain began chatting with Drew since his bed was closest to the door. Soon, she was sharing her life story with us, and Drew was who he was at heart—a pastor. She ended up asking Drew to pray a blessing over her life, which he did beautifully. I left, grinning and scratching my head. He was the one in the hospital bed, but she was asking him to pray for her!

When I returned an hour later with our lunch in hand, I walked in on what felt like a backyard bar-b-que. The roommate and his wife had pulled up chairs to sit next to Drew's bed, and everyone was talking, laughing, and encouraging one another. Drew prayed for the roommate and his wife before they left the hospital.

Was Drew in physical discomfort and bummed to be in a hospital? Absolutely. But he was also blessed and encouraged and made a difference in someone's life. We all long to know that our pain and suffering serve a higher purpose. It's about more than just us! If we scan the landscape, we'll almost certainly see those who need encouragement, compassion, and thoughtfulness.

Drew taught me to find ways to care about his cares and value his values. He cared about sharing the good news of Jesus Christ with every doctor, nurse, and roommate. That's what I care about too, so it was easy!

But there are other things that people care about for which we can be sensitive. When my mother was ill many years ago, she hated being seen without makeup. What woman wants to look terrible when people come to visit? Sometimes, the most gracious thing you can do is help someone tidy up a bit—brush her hair, dab on a bit of makeup, or help her into a fresh robe. Even a clean, colorful blanket can usher in a fresh sense of well-being. Little things mean a lot.

When helping out at someone's house, ask how you can help tidy up, make tea, and so on. This gives the patient the honor of getting to host others without doing the work. I've known people who wanted to be kept in the loop of details about school and work. The easiest way to calm someone's anxiety about the loss of control is to provide information. Give them the dignity and purpose of contributing to their life as long as possible.

One night toward the end of Drew's life, I was going to take the night shift in his home hospice care. Andy and I were at Drew's bedside as he explained the responsibilities of the evening shift.

In his southern drawl, my dignified father-in-law said, "Margaret, you're gonna have to help me pee at night, and you are going to see things you have not seen before. Are you alright with that?"

Andy chimed in and said, "Just so your things aren't bigger than my things!" We all had a good laugh, and it reminded me that many caregiving situations are ridiculous and unthinkable, but we all benefit from a hearty chuckle. Whether you laugh or cry, be gentle and kind. Keep a light heart as much as you can, even though you may be exhausted, sad, or bewildered.

Here are some practical tips for your job as a gracious caregiver:

• **Follow the adage: Put the oxygen mask on yourself first before helping others.** Most caregiving is vital and urgent and can be a life-or-death situation; however, it's not sustainable to sacrifice your mental and physical health to care for another long-term. Caregivers often battle exhaustion and discouragement. We all need gulps of fresh air to make it through difficult times, so my friend, take care of yourself as you care for others. This self-care is vital. You must take care of yourself to be any help at all to someone else. Simple things like drinking water throughout the day, going for walks, getting outside, laughing with someone, and engaging in something not health-related are lifelines for caregivers.

• **Remember, the role of Savior is already filled.** Yes, your role in caregiving is important. But you are not Jesus Christ— or the Holy Spirit. You aren't even Buddha, just to be clear. You are a human being caring for another human being. That's all.

We can get so immersed in the intensely dramatic situations revolving around keeping another human alive that we lose perspective. It reminds me of the story of Jethro, Moses' Father-in-law (Exodus 18:14-27). In the throes of Israel's delivery from Pharaoh and the Egyptians, Moses had a humanitarian crisis.

"It came about that Moses sat to judge the people, and the people stood about Moses from morning until evening."

Moses explained, "When they have a dispute, it comes to me, and I judge between a man and his neighbor and make known the statutes of God and His laws."

But Jethro observed, "The thing that you are doing is not good. You will surely wear out, both yourself

and these people who are with you, for the task is
too heavy for you; you cannot do it alone."

Jethro basically explained a plan of delegating responsibility at a crucial juncture in Israel's history and he concluded,

"If you do this thing and God so commands you,
then you will be able to endure, and all these
people also will go to their place in peace."

Moses listened to his father-in-law's advice, and everything began to run a lot smoother! As a caregiver, do what is necessary for yourself so that you will not wear out. Be gracious to yourself. Be clear about the limitations of your role and advocate for the best experience for everyone involved.

• **Nurture your hopefulness and faith.** Guard that tiny flame of faith. You and only you manage your hope and faith levels.

If you are feeding your spirit on "Grey's Anatomy" and other medical dramas, your faith levels will take a hit. Encourage yourself in the Lord so that you can offer what your patient longs for—a refreshing drink of hope, love, and power.

Your patient needs the best of you—your joy, hope, and conviction. Your patient needs to hear what God is saying to you and for you to share His perspective. Don't let anything detract from that ministry.

• **Pray prayers that bring about change.** Scripture tells us, "Elijah was a man with a nature like ours, and he prayed earnestly that it would not rain, and it did not rain on the earth for three years and six months" (James 5:17).

Our prayers are powerful, and they have a purpose. For thousands of years, the church has understood that it is Satan who kills, steals, and destroys. But in the last 200 years, we've gotten it backward. Now we say that God caused someone's cancer, or He "allowed" it. If God "allowed" someone's illness, wouldn't that mean it is His will, and then why would we seek medical help to get out of His will? No, my friend, I only see Jesus healing sickness in the Bible, not causing it. Pray fervently for healing, deliverance, salvation, and wholeness. Your prayers make a difference!

Stand in those sacred spaces, bringing casseroles and rides and presence, along with a warrior spirit. Fight the enemy on behalf of your loved one. God longs to partner with our faith to bring life abundantly. God will honor our prayers to change atmospheres and outcomes. Remember that even in the darkest circumstances, God's love is real. He is good even when we don't understand everything around us.

The Other Faces of Caregiving

There are many facets of caring for folks. My amazing friend, Misty, cares for foster children in her home. She has three of her seven biological children still living with her and a steady flow of foster kids coming in and out. In one month, she cared for twenty-five foster children!

"How do you make dinner for all these children when you don't even know how many you might host that day?" I once asked. "Dinner is no big deal," she replied. "The hard part is how isolated I feel."

In a soul-baring moment, Misty explained that no one wants to draw near to a chaotic situation. People worry that her kids might be troubled, or they don't want to invest in someone who is only there temporarily. She also shared that many more women are working now and don't have time to come alongside her. I was honestly surprised to hear that, in general, Misty does this work alone. Few people offer to provide a meal, take the kids to the park or doctor appointments, help with laundry, or ease any of the tedious workload associated with caring for so many children.

Another surprise was hearing every foster parent's frustration when people comment, "Oh, I couldn't do foster care; it would break my heart!" Exasperated, Misty said, "Do I look like I'm made of steel? Of course, it's difficult and painful! Of course, my heart breaks over these kids, especially the ones who live with us for months! But that doesn't change our calling to care for society's least, last, and lost."

Misty taught me some simple lessons about gracious caregiving through her heroic care of foster children:

• **Support groups are essential to our success.** Misty found a Facebook® support group that helps bridge the isolation. It has encouraged and sustained her to talk with folks online who understand the ins and outs of foster care. She's also connected with an organization called Fostering Hope that helps provide needed clothing and personal items for the kids.

Think about the comfort we receive from God as a precise, gracious, and beautiful tool to comfort others. "God… who comforts us in all our affliction so that we will be able to comfort those who are in any affliction with the comfort with which we ourselves are comforted by God" (2 Corinthians 1:4). Everything we receive from God is a gracious gift to share with someone else.

• **Boundaries must exist alongside compassion.** It is because of Misty's great care for children that she sometimes has to say *no* to a new placement. She can't bring a violent teen into her home when it's filled with small children. She has learned to have clear boundaries of how much she can safely manage. Compassion runs strong, but like Misty, we must employ healthy, wise boundaries.

• **Keep your eyes open for the needs around you.** You may not be able to take foster kids into your home, but you can drop off a meal to someone who does, do loads of laundry, or clean the house. Any caretaker of special-needs kids would appreciate a night off. And think about the single moms and dads you know. Helping them with driving for after-school activities would be a blessing.

Philippians 2:3-4 tells us, "…with humility of mind regard one another as more important than yourselves; do not merely look out for your own personal interests, but also for the interests of others." It's assumed that we will take care of our personal interests, but the Apostle Paul was noting that gracious Christ-followers don't merely do just that; they care with the same excellence and attention for the needs of others. It's who we are.

As you enter into that sacred space of caring for another—laying down your fears, your schedule, and in many ways, your heart—Jesus Christ, the Risen Son of God draws near to you. He says, "Peace I leave with you; My peace I give to you; not as the world gives, do I give to you. Do not let your heart be troubled, nor let it be fearful." (John 14:27).

As a loving parent to a hurting child, Jesus says, "Come to Me, all who are weary and heavy-laden, and I will give you rest" (Matthew 11:28). In those crazy, chaotic moments of caregiving, when we feel isolated and afraid—and our prayers seem to bounce off the ceiling—grab hold of His lifeline and know God cares, God sees, God is near. We can graciously care for others because He is so careful with us.

Meaningful Dialogue

1. How have you have received care and given care? Describe what that was like for you.

2. How can you rely on the Holy Spirit while caring for others? Do you sense a partnership with Him, or do you feel all alone in caregiving?

3. How can you encourage yourself and others involved in caregiving?

4. Because this process sometimes involves loss, is there anyone you need to forgive or release to God?

Declarations for Gracious Living

I have all the strength I need! I can keep on doing all things through Christ who keeps on strengthening me. (Philippians 4:13)

I have peace unlike what the world gives. (John 14:27)

I have perfect peace because my mind is set on God. (Isaiah 26:3)

God knows the plans He has for me and those plans are for my good. (Jeremiah 29:11)

PART TWO

Reaching Out

"It's in Christ that we find out who we are and what we are living for. Long before we first heard of Christ and got our hopes up, he had his eye on us, had designs on us for glorious living, part of the overall purpose he is working out in everything and everyone."

EPHESIANS 1:11-12

8

Churchy Girls

"I write so that you will know how one ought to conduct himself in the household of God, which is the church of the living God, the pillar and support of the truth."
1 TIMOTHY 3:15

Leigh loved being the life of the party. When she met Tony, a handsome police officer, they instantly became the center of a large group of friends. Weekends were spent partying at the lake with several boats and jet skis in the mix. Looking back on that time in their relationship, Leigh described their life as hard and fast.

Tony and Leigh married and soon discovered they were pregnant. Their life needed to change, but Tony didn't want to ditch the party scene. By the time their daughter was three, Leigh was a single mom. For the first time in her life, she felt lonely and feared her future. As she struggled to make ends meet each month, a mom from her daughter's daycare center invited Leigh to church. She decided to give it a try, even though attending church had never before entered her mind. Leigh shared the following with me.

"My first impression was that the people seemed plain compared to the friends I was used to. But they felt real. I thought they would judge all my tattoos, but the women I met were solidly genuine. I felt myself relax when I was with them. I started going to a Bible study and learning how to base my identity on who Jesus said I am—and not what anyone else thought I should be. At the end of the Bible study, someone asked me if I wanted to be born again and live the rest of my life with Jesus as my Lord. I practically yelled, "Yes!" and we all started laughing and crying.

"Since then, my life has completely changed. I have true friends. The most genuine and caring people cherish my daughter and teach her about the love of God in a way I never had growing up. Where I felt lonely and afraid, now I feel surrounded and protected.

"The first time I heard 1 Peter 2:9, 'But you are a chosen race, a royal priesthood, a holy nation, a people for God's own possession, so that you may proclaim the excellencies of Him who has called you out of darkness in His marvelous light,' in my heart I said yes—that's what Jesus has done for me. He called me out of darkness and emptiness and into His beautiful light, and I'm so thankful. The church had every reason to look down at me with my foul mouth. Instead, they took my daughter and me in and loved us like we were family!"

Sure, you may say, "That's a beautiful story, Margaret, but I've seen church members act horribly toward non-believers and nearly come to blows over parking spaces, or carpet color, or music styles!"

God's church on this earth is not perfect, far from it. But, praise God, one day it will be! The church, God's glorious church, will one day be united and pure, and elicit a sigh of satisfaction and praise we have missed our entire lives.

But for now, God calls us to come alongside people in a gracious and supportive way. Each of us must make that conscious choice every time we enter a church. Throughout trials, heartaches, and all the tedious work, we see God's redeeming love. People grow; they pick up the pieces and make new lives. That's beauty from ashes. That's the church in living color!

Since we're already wearing our best clothes and flashing bright smiles, what does graciousness look like in our beautiful communities of faith? Well, it's intentional, energetic, and focused. Here's everyday wisdom for graciously embracing those you interact with on Sunday—and why doing so is a huge deal.

Everybody is Messed Up

Sometimes, church can leave a bad taste in your mouth. Call it an oversight or a lack of professionalism. Chalk it up to small-town ways or start-up growing pains. Or call it what it is: humanity. Maybe the nursery isn't run well, a Sunday school teacher is rude, people are judgmental, or the pastor contradicts known science. Remember what I said in chapter one: "We all tangle with mean-spirited, small-minded, judgmental chicks in church." Yep, that's often the reality.

But we can overlook and overcome. I know this will come as no great surprise, but everybody is messed up and in dire need of grace! There is no perfect church because every human attending it is messed up. We need to get over ourselves and our unrealistic expectations about church and do our best to love and honor folks.

The Apostle Paul wrote to Timothy: "I write so that you will know how one ought to conduct himself in the household of God, which is the church of the living God, the pillar and support of the truth" (1 Timothy 3:15). We all need instruction on how we should conduct ourselves in the household of God. Why is that? Because it matters!

As imperfect and jacked up as it is, our gathering of Christ-followers is called the "church of the living God." We are representing the King of all kings and His reign on earth. It's a big deal. That's why we are told, "Be on guard for yourselves and for all the flock, among which the Holy Spirit has made you overseers, to shepherd the church of God which He purchased with His own blood" (Acts 20:28).

What an assignment! The Holy Spirit assigned overseers for something precious and purchased by Christ's blood: the church. God designed His church to be a light in the darkness, a seasoning for the world. Who we are as a community is far-reaching! If we, the church, don't display the love of God, who will?

I love the way, *The Message* phrases Romans 12:16-17. "Laugh with your happy friends when they're happy; share tears when they're down. Get along with each other; don't be stuck up. Make friends with nobodies; don't be the great somebody. Don't hit back; discover beauty in everyone." Those are gracious marching orders for churchgoers!

When you encounter a slip-up at church, an oversight or thoughtless gesture, choose to be gracious. The church is run primarily by volunteers, so be gentle and loving with their humanity in mind. You can hope for courteous behavior, but there's an intentional rhythm to graciousness. Seeing the same folks every week and caring for one another through life's ups and downs—and those not-so-pretty moments—is part of that.

That's one reason we are to pray without ceasing, my friend! Prayer is a beautiful, gracious act. Knowing that church folks are praying for you and that you are praying for them builds an invisible bond.

Graciousness also rises in other unexpected ways, such as excellence and professionalism in doing quality work, even as a volunteer. Graciousness looks like inclusion on every level and offers opportunities for everyone to contribute. There isn't an "us" or "them" in God's church, or at least there shouldn't be. We are on the same team, working together to create good.

We showcase graciousness through appropriate affection and warmth to everyone we encounter. Romans 12:10 tells us, "Love from the center of who you are; don't fake it. Run for dear life from evil; hold on for dear life to good. Be good friends who love deeply; practice playing second fiddle." If we live these words out loud at church, the whole world will hear!

Never Judge from the Outside

I remember hearing a pastor tell of a service in which a woman seated behind him was sobbing and almost screaming. He refrained from turning around to ask her to get control of herself. Afterward, he learned God had dramatically healed her during the service from a recent sexual-assault trauma.

We must never judge from the outside what God is doing in someone's heart. We are not the junior Holy Spirit, convicting others of righteousness and sin. Trust God to do that work in others. Many times, I've struggled with a fellow believer's behavior only to find out soon enough that the Holy Spirit was speaking to that individual.

Surely church is a place where we can cry our tears and pour out our hearts to God without the judgment of others. Graciousness shows up in honoring someone's spiritual experience because church truly is mysterious, holy ground.

Folks may cry at church, and they also may laugh with joy or want to dance and sing. Graciousness does not distract or judge. Great questions to ask someone in your church include:

What is God doing in your life right now?

What are some of the ways God is growing you in this season?

How can I pray for you?

How can I encourage and support you?

One of the secrets of gracious living is to remember that all behavior makes sense. If someone looks frustrated, angry, or depressed, there's a reason behind it. Be gracious and tread lightly.

Speak Life

When I see believers arguing and fighting over non-essential matters, I ache. We can extend gracious honor to those whose opinions differ from ours on biblical interpretation and how to live the Christian life. Such graciousness transforms the way we talk about church and one another.

Come on now, do you roast the pastor's sermon as soon as you get in your car? Roasting to ridiculing your church community certainly doesn't reflect a gracious spirit. I once heard this Texas adage: "Any jackass can kick a barn down, but it takes a carpenter to build one!"

I realize it's easy to criticize the church, but it requires time and skill to create a thoughtful experience. Bless and build up your church, its people, and your pastoral staff. How about other denominations and Christians who don't quite see things the way you do? Bless them! Pray for them and know that God will work in their minds and hearts.

It's wise to regularly ask yourself, *Will the world truly know me and my fellow church members by the love we have for one another?* If things aren't going the way you'd like, seek out ways to contribute rather than complain. Remember that death and life are in the power of the tongue (Proverbs 18:21). Rather than cursing and criticizing other believers, speak life over them. Ask God to bless, encourage, prosper, and fulfill them. My friend, you will build honor for yourself and them when you speak life instead of criticism.

Embrace Restoration

When I worked in campus ministry at San Jose State University, a racially diverse campus, our Bible studies attracted only ten to fifteen students—until I advertised a study to be led by a friend of mine with the last name of Nguyen. Then, we suddenly had fifty ethnically diverse students show up! It was fantastic!

As a church body, we must acknowledge our role in racism and actively seek restoration in our churches and country. What other community holds such redemptive potential as the church? Black, white, and brown worshipping God together and calling one another brother and sister is the church at its purest. How encouraging it is to walk into my church and not see a dominant color! There are equal numbers of all ethnic groups in the congregation, as well as the staff. It's beautiful!

I believe that true revival and authentic Christianity erase racism. The Azusa Street Revival illustrates this point. It exploded on the scene in Los Angeles in 1906, led by William J. Seymour, an African American preacher. Seymour, a son of slaves, welcomed men, women, and children of all races. The revival continued until 1915 and is considered the most significant revival of the century. Frank Bartleman, a pastor and writer at the time, enthusiastically exclaimed, "The color line was washed away in the blood."[14]

Yes, this washing is what happens when we live out Galatians 3:28: "There is neither Jew nor Greek, there is neither slave nor free man, there is neither male nor female; for you are all one in Christ Jesus."

The restorative ministry potential of the church to walk in racial reconciliation is unlimited. Yes, the church, crafted from every tribe, tongue, and nation, is the beautiful and gracious representation of Jesus loving this world.

Savor the Investment

Here's what I love about church: It's a no-brainer—a weekly investment in our emotional and spiritual health. And it's free! Who doesn't want that?

Every week, a plumb line stretches across our lives, our hopes and dreams, relationships, lifestyles, and habits. Everything measures against the straight edge of God's glorious presence. When I've been short-tempered with the kids, a song, a sentence from a sermon, or just entering the sweet presence of God helps me. I became instantly aware of my temper and swap it out for a softer approach.

That kind of therapy magic happens almost every week. And, remember, it's free! Church is the oasis where I lay down my burdens and sit at Jesus' feet. When Christ said, "Come to

Me, all who are weary and heavy-laden, and I will give you rest" (Matthew 11:28), He meant it. He was also releasing a spiritual truth for all time: our hearts change from weary and burdened to light and peaceful when we enter the presence of God.

Provide a Loving, Peaceful Place for Your Children

Recently during a church service, I glanced down the row of seats to behold my four beautiful children. With their hands raised and faces turned upward to God, they were totally enraptured in worship. It was a precious moment when all seemed right in the world.

A note to all you young moms out there: in twenty years, your kids may share that their favorite church memories were snuggling with you on the pew while coloring. Graciousness at church might mean denying your own need for a few moments of peace with God and simply being close to a little one.

And here's another reality: church is probably the only time our kids see us sit still! I remember sitting closely with my mother as a high schooler and trying on her rings during the sermon. Church was the rare occasion I experienced my mom not moving, and I loved the closeness and stillness snuggled next to her.

My family loves church because it is a place of beauty and community. Mark your church time as a gracious, loving, peaceful space for your family. I appreciate how Jessica Smartt put it in her E-book:

> *"As a mother, most Sundays, instead of a gift I receive, church is a gift I give. A gift to the Lord—obeying Him in honoring His day. A gift to my husband and other Christians, in worshipping with them. And to my children, of course. Know*

*this, mama: when you're frustrated from dealing
with a loud or cranky little one in church, you are
not alone. You are doing the right thing!"*[16]

No Excuses: Show Up

What do you do if your church isn't a restful place? What if
you drive away feeling more annoyed than peaceful? Or confused or sad or any other possible emotion that arises when
knot-heads, I mean, broken humans, get together to worship
God? You've heard this conversation between a mother and
her son:

> *"Mom, I don't want to go to church! The people are
> mean, and they make fun of me!"*
>
> *The mother replies: "I'll give you three reasons why
> you need to go to church son: one, you are 45 years
> old, two, you need to be there, and three, you're the
> pastor!"*

But seriously, I don't think it's going to fly to stand before
God Almighty one day with the excuse, *I didn't go to church
because of the people there.* You see, each of us steward our
heart and responses in life.

In the wild-and-crazy Pentecostal megachurch I attend,
someone thought it would be a good idea to build a screen
the size of a barn and project pulsating geometric patterns
across it during worship. I keep my eyes closed to avoid the
dizziness it induces. Sometimes our music is so loud, I think
my ears will bleed; however, it remains my responsibility to
steward my heart toward God. Jesus is still saying, *Come unto
Me, Margaret, enter My friendship and conversation, whether
church is a whispered, museum-quality affair or a boisterous*

conga line, Come to Me! I long to extend My grace to you and grow you as a gracious woman.

Before you resort to the mindset, *I'm just going to worship at home*, remember 1 Peter 2:10-12:

> *"For you once were not a people, but now you are the people of God; you had not received mercy, but now you have received mercy. Beloved, I urge you as aliens and strangers to abstain from fleshly lusts which wage war against the soul. Keep your behavior excellent among the Gentiles, so that in the thing in which they slander you as evildoers, they may because of your good deeds, as they observe them, glorify God in the day of visitation."*

God Himself gathered us to become His people – and that community, when observed, reflects the glory of God.

How utterly amazing to think you can visit almost any town in most of the world and instantly connect with believers in the family of God. Community is a precious gift never to be taken for granted. Layer on top of it a connection spanning generations and socio-economic differences. And here's the cherry on top: together we forge change in the darkest corners of the world through service and generosity. The gates of hell will not prevail against it!

So, no excuses. Show up to glorify God.

Be Watchful

Sadly, sometimes there is downright evil in the church, but that should come as no surprise. Jesus warned about it through a parable in Matthew 13:24-30:

> *"The kingdom of heaven may be compared to a man who sowed good seed in his field. But while*

*his men were sleeping, his enemy came and sowed
tares among the wheat, and went away. But when
the wheat sprouted and bore grain, then the tares
became evident also. The slaves of the landowner
came and said to him, 'Sir, did you not sow good
seed in your field? How then does it have tares?'
And he said to them, 'An enemy has done this!'
The slaves said to him, 'Do you want us, then, to
go and gather them up?' But he said, 'No: for while
you are gathering up the tares, you many uproot
the wheat with them. Allow both to grow together
until the harvest; and in the time of the harvest I
will say to the reapers, 'First gather up the tares
and bind them in bundles to burn them up; but
gather the wheat into my barn. Allow both to grow
together!'"*

Do you understand this parable? Lucky for us, Jesus explained it to the disciples in Matthew 13:36-43:

*"The one who sows the good seed is the Son of
Man, and the field is the world; and as for the good
seed, these are the sons of the kingdom; and the
tares are the sons of the evil one; and the enemy
who sowed them is the devil, and the harvest is the
end of the age; and the reapers are angels. So just
as the tares are gathered up and burned with fire,
so shall it be at the end of the age. The Son of Man
will send forth His angels, and they will gather out
of His kingdom all stumbling blocks, and those
who commit lawlessness, and will throw them
into the furnace of fire; in that place there will be
weeping and gnashing of teeth."*

Yes, in the church, there are tares among the wheat.
Sometimes, we can't tell which one is which until time dis-

plays their fruit. Indeed, there are demonic powers seated in the pews of our churches! As Jesus said, the enemy plants "stumbling blocks and those who commit lawlessness." Isn't this part of what fuels the dysfunction and harm in the body of Christ? Why do you think many church pastors must hire personal bodyguards and security for the church? I remember a pastor telling me years ago that a local Wiccan had assigned people to come to our church services to pray disruption and chaos! Don't be afraid. Don't be offended. Be prayerful and watchful.

When you encounter real evil—sexual predators posing as ministers, robbers of church resources, malicious gossips, and adulterers—your first work is in the spiritual realm. Pray that God will uproot anything planted in your church that He didn't plant. Pray that evil will be thwarted and removed. Go through the proper channels of authority in your church, your denomination, and local authorities if you have serious concerns.

How sad that church must come with such a warning! We know the church is not a gathering of perfect people. But can we hold our brokenness in one hand and still reach for the church we long for? A refuge. A warm place full of comfort and beauty, creating and consuming, loving and laughing, tasting and working. Can we acknowledge harsh reality yet still hunger for the pure and sweet? Yes, we can.

Primed with Gracious Purpose

The church is not about the cold, brick building; it's about the loving relationships anchored there. The church is centered in community, which all of us need, but especially when we're hurting, confused, and lost. Any time we experience heartache and trouble, the church community rallies nearby. "Study after study shows that having a good support network constitutes the single most powerful protection against becoming traumatized. Safety and terror are incompatible."[16]

We help each other weather the storms of life. And when we do experience trauma and loss, our church community wraps arms around us like no other.

> *"Traumatized human beings recover in the context of relationships: with families, loved ones, AA meetings, veterans' organizations, religious communities, or professional therapists. The role of those relationships is to provide physical and emotional safety, including safety from feeling shamed, admonished, or judged, and to bolster the courage to tolerate, face, and process the reality of what has happened."*[17]

The ultimate purpose of the church is that while we love and grace each other in the household of faith, a watching world is won or lost for Christ! God has pieced us together as a people with a purpose: together, we demonstrate His love on earth.

Jessica Smartt concludes her book, *Memory Making Mom*, with this beautiful, gracious wisdom:

> *"What I love about the gospel is that it makes everything mean more, not less. It's not just about serving dinner to someone who needs it—it's about bringing hope to another soul who will live forever in eternity. It's not just about laughing together on a family adventure—it's about imparting value to little lives who can literally make ripples in the pond of eternity."*[18]

We, the church, are Christ's body on display. We represent Him to a watching world. When we do it right, people run to join us. They are loved and accepted, known, and understood. Destiny is called forward rather than shame. As Leigh and countless others have discovered, there's food, love, laughter, tears, and real healing—so much so that we have to get in a boat and push away from shore to speak to the crowd. Church is a place vibrant with compassion, joy, and the real stuff of life. No other community holds such redemptive purpose as God's glorious church. Don't miss out!

Meaningful Dialogue

1. Think about your history with church. Have there been positive or negative experiences that shape how you approach church?

2. How can you bring a more gracious atmosphere into your church?

3. Has your church experience been touched by judging or criticizing? How do you combat these attitudes?

4. What examples come to mind of gracious people within your church who love and serve others?

5. What are ways you can participate in bringing God's glorious church to your community of friends, neighbors, and coworkers?

Declarations for Gracious Living

The kingdom of God is at hand. I will be about His work. (Mark 1:15)

I will let my light shine to bring glory to God. (Matthew 5:16)

I am a royal priesthood, a people for God's own possession! (1Peter 2:9)

9

The Welcome Mat

"And Levi gave a big reception for Him in his house."
LUKE 5:29

Regina's house lights typically beckoned with a warm glow
on our Bible-study dinner nights. But on one particular rain-
drenched evening, the house was dark.

My friends and I used our cell-phone flashlights to pick our
way around the water puddles to the front door. We had the
habit of just walking into Regina's home. She would usually
be in the kitchen at the back of the house, looking utterly gorgeous while putting finishing touches on homemade Italian
dishes for us.

After shaking off at the front door, we walked in on what
can only be described as an "I Love Lucy" scene: Regina was
on her hands and knees in a kitchen that looked like a spa-
ghetti-sauce bomb had detonated. Red sludge spattered everything—from the cabinets to the floor to Regina's hair. Her

white Maltese poodle was licking the spattered floor and had tracked tiny blood-red paw prints throughout the kitchen.

For a few seconds, our usually chatty mouths gaped open in stunned silence, and I would've laughed, but upon seeing us, Regina burst into tears. We quickly shifted into rescue mode, lifting our friend from the floor, and whirling around that kitchen like scrubbing-bubble ninjas — cleaning the dog, the cabinets, and the floor while hitting speed-dial for pizza delivery. In those seeing-red-everywhere moments, none of us could have imagined what a beautiful gift that sauce bomb would become.

When we finally gathered around the table, sweaty but satisfied that we had conquered the sauce, our leader gently asked Regina to tell us what was happening for her that night. She described getting home later than planned, and in her rush to blend the ingredients for the sauce, she hadn't put the lid on the blender. Exhausted, she quietly said, "I try so hard to be this perfect woman, and when you guys walked in, I realized I couldn't do it anymore. I can't be what everybody thinks I'm supposed to be!"

What ensued was the most vulnerable and honest discussion we'd ever had. Laments about disappointing people, wanting things to be perfect, letting stress and image take precedence over relationships bubbled through our conversation. Deep down, Regina felt we must be disappointed in her and would, in some way, withdraw our respect or affection. Nothing could have been farther from the truth! Now we often laugh and say, "We need another spaghetti bomb to go off; things are getting too tidy and predictable!"

That moment of imperfection and vulnerability—that beautiful, in-your-face, red mess—drew us together. In contrast, the image of Regina as the perfect host had kept us apart.

I had often left Regina's home requesting a recipe but never asking for prayer. Unconsciously I had surmised *How could I bring my hurts and fears into that Martha-Stewart setting?*

The Problem with Perfection

Don't we all love to project an image of having it together! That pristine mindset often stifles the desire to host others in our homes. We shudder when we think about having to rise to a hosting occasion. So much to do. So little time. Even less energy. Deep sigh. Has hosting others always been so stressful?

But before we let guilt propel us to sweep off our welcome mats and give hospitality another shot, let's take a peek at Scripture. You see, gracious hospitality is a biblical gig, and many of us have been doing it the hard way for years, which is why we're more prone to avoid it all together these days.

We're told to "be hospitable to one another without complaint" (1 Peter 4:9). That's not a suggestion, my friend. It's a mandate that, believe it or not, is good for guests and hosts. Stay with me!

Luke 10 gives us an intimate snapshot of first-century hospitality and some of the struggles that went with it, including cooking a meal without electricity or an Instapot®!

Here's the scenario: A woman welcomed Jesus into her home. Her heart of hospitality beat with a warm welcome. Her sister was seated at the guest's feet, listening to every word He spoke. But the first woman, the welcoming host, "was distracted with all her preparations; and she came up to Him and said, 'Lord, do You not care that my sister has left me to do all the serving alone? Then tell her to help me'" (Luke 10:40).

Martha welcomed Jesus into her home and sought to worship through her service. Martha's experience was not so peaceful, though. The Greek word that is translated distracted in the NASB means "to be drawn different ways at the same time." Martha was so busy doing things, she forgot about being present for her guest. In contrast, her sister, Mary, had assumed a position reserved for disciples: She was seated at the feet of Jesus listening. She was worshiping Him through her presence and attention.

I love the tender heart of Jesus. He gently said His host's name after she had whined about Mary taking a seat when she needed her in the kitchen. "Martha, Martha, you are worried and bothered about so many things, but only one thing is necessary, for Mary has chosen the good part, which shall not be taken away from her" (vv. 41-42).

What's the one necessary thing for a gracious host? Jesus wasn't saying, "One entree is enough, Martha." He was saying. "Sweet Martha, the one thing that matters is your relationship with Me."

You see, Jesus came to call us friends, not servants (John 15:15). Martha was living the posture of a servant rather than a friend of Jesus. Fast-forward to today, and we gals still get that out of order, don't we?

In hosting, we typically touch a guest with one hand and hold a dishtowel in the other. But we must find the balance between focusing on our guests and getting things done. Perhaps Martha discovered, as my friend Regina did, that serving is an unfulfilling substitute for the intimacy, vulnerability, and humility required of genuine relationship.

Beautiful messes can indeed open our eyes to truth. And speaking of that, the most gracious hosts I've encountered live in impoverished areas of India, Peru, and Haiti, where there were no stunning floral centerpieces. Sometimes, there were no tables!

One summer, our family traveled to India to meet a group of girls we are helping to educate for college. We were excited to be together, but the heat and humidity, combined with jet lag, wilted my crew by three in the afternoon. Miraculously, at the perfect time, our hosts would emerge with little cups of chai. The girls would place our chairs underneath a fan so we could cool off while we drank. It was a simple setting of plastic chairs and a concrete floor, but thoughtfulness and honor reigned, so we felt like royalty at a palace! Their kindness humbled me, and I reflected on the attention I had given (or failed to provide) guests in my cushy American home. The hosting skills of those girls were simple but rich in friendship and love—just the way Jesus taught gracious hospitality. Relationship accented—not dominated—by service. Could it be that gracious hosting is as simple as a cup of tea and a little time?

If you—like Regina, Martha, and me—have started as a gracious host with a welcoming heart but ended in frustration and exhaustion, it's time to boot the perfection idol! We start out wanting to host people because we genuinely care about them, and we want to represent Christ to the world. Like Martha in the Luke 10 passage, we so easily fall into the trap of caring more about serving than relating. It starts with a heart to honor someone by presenting well. But before you can pop open a bottle of Martinelli's cider, you're engrossed in elaborate recipes, fancy trays, flower arrangements, and cleaning out drawers no one will ever open.

"Martha, Martha (fill in your name here), you are worried and distracted about so many things." Be a gracious host by releasing every distraction. I like Charlotte Shultz's advice. As the wife of former Secretary of State George Schultz, she has hosted every VIP visiting the San Francisco Bay area, hosting beautifully but always mindful of honoring the people who enter her home. Her simple hosting routine? "Greet guests at the door; get them a drink. Plan everything, and once the party starts, forget it. It's too late to do anything else."

So, soak up the loving words of Jesus and enjoy your guests, my friend! People value your thoughtful attentiveness more than any artful centerpiece or elaborate menu. I prefer a peaceful, happy host over a nervous perfectionist any day. Keep clear on your priorities. Pleasant wins over perfect!

And speaking of the beauty of imperfection, can you recall the last time you sat at a friend's kitchen table, talking over a cup of homemade coffee or tea? I miss the intimacy of those kitchen-table times. Yes, it's easier to meet at Starbucks, but it costs us a lot more than we think. These days, we're losing the value of quiet conversations, the emotional capacity to host, and the beautiful mess of vulnerability. We are losing the story of "this is us" as we slide into the isolation of keeping others out and our doors shut because of what? Dishes piled in the kitchen sink? Shoes littering the hallway? Dog hair on the carpet? Who cares? That's real life! Yet, we are unaccustomed to the vulnerability of letting others into our personal space, and thus we continue on a trajectory toward isolation.

Sometimes, fear of judgment and rejection keeps us from opening our homes to others. *Is my backyard landscaped as well as yours? Is my house clean enough, beautiful enough, decorated enough, enough, enough, enough?* And so, our insecurity focuses our eyes on self and not on others. It robs us of the intimacy and vulnerability of conversations around a kitchen table.

But know this, my friend: You are enough as you are. Your kitchen table is sufficient to welcome someone into your home and heart. You don't need Starbucks' plastic chairs and the ricocheting conversations of other coffee addicts. You only need yourself, your kitchen table, a pot of homemade coffee, and an invited friend to make a difference in her life and yours. And goodness gracious, what a difference a kitchen conversation can make! So, do it even though there are dishes in the sink and dust balls are floating on your hardwood floors. Forget perfection and embrace relationship.

Check Your Respect & Humility

Here's a hospitality story on the opposite end of the spectrum from Martha's situation. Luke 7:36-50 tells the story of a Pharisee named Simon who invited Jesus to dinner at his home but showed little respect for Him. A woman of the street came in, wet the feet of Jesus with her tears, wiped them with her hair, and anointed Jesus with perfume.

In verse 44, Jesus said to Simon, "Do you see this woman? I entered your house; you gave Me no water for My feet, but she has wet My feet with her tears and wiped them with her hair. You gave Me no kiss; but she, since the time I came in, has not ceased to kiss My feet. You did not anoint My head with oil, but she anointed My feet with perfume."

No water. No kiss. No oil. What did that utter failure to provide basic kindness mean? It seems a prideful spirit supplanted any good intention of Simon's hospitality. Common courtesy in that dusty region was to offer water to wash one's feet before reclining at the table. Simon withheld this service. He didn't even greet Jesus in a friendly manner of kissing each cheek. Oil on the head was a sign of blessing and deference; Simon withheld that too.

If I were guessing, I would say Simon wasn't a sincere seeker but had merely invited Jesus over to position himself in the middle of the activity. Perhaps he didn't offer these common courtesies or basic respect fearing that others would think he overly honored the rebel rabbi.

If it's exhausting to care too much about what people think when visiting our homes, it's equally draining to carry a low opinion of our guests. If you find yourself put out with hosting, take a quiet look at your honor and respect for your guests. Are they an imposition? Is it possible that you've partnered with resentment while feigning hospitality? Are you merely positioning yourself to be in the middle of the action? Do you desire more to impress than bless? Or maybe, like Simon, you're trying to do "the right thing" by hosting, but your heart's not in it. No one else will have the youth group over after church, so you offer—grudgingly. But rather than praying how to bless those kids, you're churning *How can I keep my carpets white?* It's easy to see how no water, no kiss, and no oil came about! Don't host out of obligation or pride. These are all valid heart checks if you often host people without joy in your heart.

The truth is humility shapes gracious hosting. If I feel superior to my guests, then it makes sense to offer leftovers because, in some way, I'm doing them a favor, and I think it's enough. But when humility leads me to bestow honor on my guests, it makes sense to offer them my best, which doesn't have to be elaborate. My best can be a cup of chai while I'm sitting in a plastic chair under a fan— or having decaf coffee available because I know that's what guests prefer. Or, it can be having someone's favorite playlist humming on the stereo. Thoughtfulness goes a long way toward making someone feel welcomed and valued.

Missing Out

Ever wonder what we're missing when we aren't hospitable? Let's check out a story that paints a picture of the full circle of hosting. In 2 Kings 4:8-37, a Shunammite woman interacted with the prophet Elisha over many years. Their relationship began when the woman persuaded him to stay in her home. Scripture says that it became a habit for him to always enjoy a homecooked meal there.

She may have been a good cook and great company, or perhaps the woman was simply welcoming! She recognized Elisha was a holy man of God and that he passed by frequently. So, she said to her husband, "Please, let us make a little walled upper chamber and let us set a bed for him there, and a table and a chair and a lampstand; and it shall be, when he comes to us, that he can turn in there" (v. 10).

They built a room exclusively for Elisha, and he rested there and responded by saying, "Behold you have been careful for us with all this care; what can I do for you?" (v. 13). He offered to lift her before the king and the captain of the army, but she did not want or need such accolades.

However, when Elisha discovered the woman had no son, he proclaimed that by the next year she would have one. It happened just as Elisha prophesied. But when the child was older and working with his father in the field, he became ill and was carried home, where he died. His mother laid him on the prophet's bed in the upper chamber and closed the door. She acted as if nothing had happened! Then she saddled up her donkey and hauled ass (sorry I couldn't help it) to the prophet's house, telling her husband and Elisha's servant, "everything is fine."

But when the Shunammite woman found the man of God, she grabbed hold of Elisha's feet and said she would not leave him. Elisha ran to her house and prayed for her son. "He then laid on the child, putting his mouth on his mouth and his eyes on his eyes and his hands on his hands, and he stretched himself on him, and the flesh of the child became warm" (v. 34). Elisha paced in the house and then laid on the child again till the boy sneezed seven times and opened his eyes. The prophet then presented the boy back to his mom alive, and the Shunammite woman "fell at his feet and bowed to the ground and took her son and went out" (v. 37).

That's a great story tucked into a chapter packed with so many lessons! And isn't that what hospitality frequently presents to us? Often, it's a terrific story tucked into a chapter of life. There are twists and turns, sometimes unspoken dreams that come to be, along with encounters with God—and perhaps moments of desperation and awe! It's what we build room for in our lives. If we build space for the things of God, He will bless us. If we construct walls of pride and selfishness, we will eat their bitter fruits. What you build will return itself to you, my friend.

The Shunammite woman saw a need and perceived the presence of God. She didn't just throw a sleeping bag on a floor; she built a room and furnished it with what Elisha needed: a bed, a table and chair, and a lamp. Her gracious and thoughtful hospitality opened her up to a lifelong relationship. Elisha demonstrated his commitment to her well-being throughout the layers of navigating the healing of her son.

But the story does not end there! The woman is mentioned again in 2 Kings 8:1-6. Elisha warned her of a seven-year famine that was coming. She escaped because of his warning, and when she returned, Elisha's servant had just been speaking of her to the king. So, the king proclaimed, "Restore all that was hers and all the produce of the field from the day that she left and the land even until now" (v. 6).

Think about it! This woman graciously hosted Elisha by feeding him and setting up a room. Their lifelong friendship won her a son and the preservation of their family throughout a famine. We never know which small gestures of gracious kindness will boomerang into our lives more goodness, protection, and blessing.

The Presence of Christ

Often gracious hospitality is the opening up, not just of our homes, but our lives. How can we love our neighbors as ourselves if we don't even know them, much less host them in our homes? Perhaps that's why the New Testament frequently describes a Christ-follower as one who shows hospitality.

The qualification for being an elder in the first-century church was, among other things, to be hospitable (Titus 1:8; 1 Timothy 3:2). And in Hebrews 13:2, we are given this tantalizing piece of advice: "Do not neglect to show hospitality to strangers, for by this some have entertained angels without knowing it."

Is it possible that when you invite your in-laws, neighbors, school contacts, and even strangers over, heaven has visited earth? That's highly probable given what Jesus said in Matthew 25:35-36, "For I was hungry, and you gave Me something to eat; I was thirsty, and you gave Me something to drink; I was a stranger, and you invited Me in; naked, and you clothed Me; I was sick and you visited Me; I was in prison, and you came to Me." You know the story, the righteous asked, "When did we do these things for you?" The answer? "To the extent that you did it to one of these brothers of Mine, even the least of them, you did it to Me" (v. 40).

In addition to your hospitality with people, what about hosting the presence of God? How do you leave the porch light on for God? How do you welcome and honor Him?

In the Old Testament, Israel camped around God's presence. Bill Johnson, the pastor of Bethel Church in Redding California, once said, "Somehow we must adjust whatever is necessary to rediscover the practical nature of the presence of God being central to all we do and are." He added, "It's been said of the early church that ninety-five percent of their activities would have stopped had the Holy Spirit been removed from them. But it is also stated that ninety-five percent of the modern church's activities would continue as normal because there is so little recognition of His presence."[19]

Do you have a sense of God's presence in your home? Is the porch light on for Him? If you welcome and honor the presence of God in your home, everyone who enters will feel it.

I once led a women's Bible study that seemed steeped in turmoil and drama. Women would come in late or grumpy. Confusion and even animosity erupted in our discussions. Finally, my co-host suggested that we anoint the room and pray before each meeting. We anointed the door with oil, forbidding any evil presence to enter, and we welcomed the Holy Spirit to permeate our meeting. The difference was palatable!

These days, I always bless my home before people enter. I pray that the Holy Spirit will work His agenda over mine. I pray that people will be blessed, encouraged, and filled with His presence when they step foot on my property. No other spirit can enter when we have invited Christ into our homes and are honoring Him there. Of course, your home will be peaceful and beautiful if you have welcomed Christ. The true essence of being a gracious host is the presence of Christ. Welcome Him and others into your home, and you will be amazed how you will shine even if your floors do not.

Meaningful Dialogue

1. When do you feel the need to look like the picture-perfect host? How does that feel for you? How does your perfection mindset make your family and guests feel?

2. What was Mary's mindset as she hosted Jesus as contrasted to Martha's? Where do you resonate on the Mary-Martha scale?

3. Who could you bless with hospitality? What stops you from hosting others?

4. What does it look like to welcome the Holy Spirit's presence into your home and your hosting?

Declarations for Gracious Living

I entertain angels by being hospitable. (Hebrews 13:2)

I have perfect peace because I trust in You. (Isaiah 26:3)

My home is a gift from You. I am generous with all that I have. (James 1:17)

10

Working at It

"Whatever you do, do your work heartily,
as for the Lord rather than for men."

ColossIANS 3:23

After graduating from college in South Carolina, Jessica put her packaging science degree to work with a large chemical company in California, where she quickly became the project leader for several large jobs. She recalled when she excitedly traveled to one project site, anticipating a shipment of 1500 containers. However, her excitement quickly drained into dismay when the dock foreman told her the containers had not been loaded onto pallets. Jessica had 1500 containers to unload solo by hand! She chose to laugh, roll up her sleeves, and get the job done.

"Every day, I have a crazy problem to solve, and usually, it's human error," she says. "Of course, sometimes, it's mine!"

Stifling laughter, Jessica then told me about a business trip she took to Princeton, New Jersey, to oversee the start-up of a project. She arrived around midnight and drove an hour on dark, winding backroads to her hotel. Upon arriving, Jessica mapped the project site to estimate her commute the next morning. When she plugged the factory address into her mapping directions, Jessica gasped. She was laughing hard as she told me the story. "I was supposed to be in Princeton, Illinois, not *New Jersey!* I wanted to cry, but my team booked a crack-of-dawn flight for me while I frantically checked out of my hotel and raced back to the airport." Upon her return, Jessica's entire team enjoyed a celebration dinner, presenting a United States atlas as her prize.

Being part of a graciously fun company can mean the difference between a job you enjoy and one you barely tolerate. For Jessica, it's not that her work doesn't present absurd obstacles to overcome, but fascinating projects and a quick-witted team of gracious coworkers outweigh any road bumps.

Healthy teams foster excellence, along with positive cooperation and camaraderie. Jessica's team finds reasons to celebrate and spend time together with trips, dinners, and concerts. Their gracious, honest approach in the workplace keeps everyone sharp and close as friends.

Workplace Wisdom

Sadly, most of us don't waltz into a fabulous work environment or have the slightest idea what our career should be. "In a 2014 Gallup poll, more than two-thirds of adults said they were 'not engaged' at work, a good portion of whom were 'actively disengaged.'"[20]

Angela Duckworth, author of *Grit: The Power of Passion and Perseverance*, highlights the difficulty many young people face in choosing a career:

> *"To the thirty-something on Reddit with 'a fleeting interest in everything' and 'no career direction,' here's what science has to say: passion for your work is a little bit of discovery, followed by a lot of development, and then a lifetime of deepening."*[21]

In our instant-gratification, microwave culture, this is tough news to hear. It takes time to search out what fascinates us and even more time to advance and flourish.

But Duckworth stresses the importance of such discovery, development, and deepening. It seems it's the secret of gracious living in the workplace because the well-being of oneself and others is at the heart of it.

"For most people, interest without purpose is nearly impossible to sustain for a lifetime. It is imperative that you identify your work as both personally interesting and, at the same time, integrally connected to the well-being of others."[22]

I would also add a dimension of co-laboring with Christ in the workplace. We should actively seek to impact the kingdom of God through our employment. When I became a Christ-follower in high school, one of the first problems I ran into concerned work. On fire for Jesus, I thought *Why should I waste my time working when I could be out sharing the gospel?*

My mentor, Judy, straightened me out quickly with this nugget of wisdom from 2 Thessalonians 3:10: "If anyone is not willing to work, then he is not to eat, either." Judy told me to share my faith fluidly, but I still had to earn a living! That passage helped set a standard for me as a high schooler. I remember being impressed that the Bible possessed such practical instruction for everyday life that could impact the kingdom of God.

Paul also wrote, "For you yourselves know how you ought to follow our example, because we did not act in an undisciplined manner among you, nor did we eat anyone's bread without paying for it, but with labor and hardship we kept working night and day so that we would not be a burden to any of you; not because we do not have the right to this, but in order to offer ourselves as a model for you, so that you would follow our example" (2 Thessalonians 3:7-9).

After Paul's nifty proverb—*If you don't work, you don't eat*—he summed it up in verse 11: "For we hear that some among you are leading an undisciplined life, doing no work at all, but acting like busybodies."

The contrast I saw was hard work, along with thoughtful, intentional living, blessed onlookers, while undisciplined, gossipy laziness burdened those nearby. I'm so thankful for the plumb line of the Word of God that set me straight at a young age! In 2 Thessalonians 3, I peered into a well of wisdom, integrity, diligence, and graciousness concerning work and employment.

That same summer, I started my first real job as an administrative assistant for an engineering firm. My supervisor was a no-nonsense Christian woman committed to training young staff. She demanded a level of integrity and professionalism that set the bar for the entirety of my working life. Not a minute of an hour or a stamp for an envelope was mine to waste on personal interests. She instructed me that, as a Christian, I should perform my work with the utmost integrity and give my employer every minute of every hour for which I was paid, a whopping $2.65 per hour minimum wage! I learned to view work as a privilege and endeavored to do it well.

My supervisor quoted a proverb for every situation, and those words of wisdom still ring in my head:

- Whenever I was colliding with the three o'clock doldrums, her guidance pointed me toward these words: "The way of the lazy is as a hedge of thorns, but the path of the upright is a highway" (Proverbs 15:19).

- To keep me focused on excellence, I was reminded of Proverbs 22:29: "Do you see a man skilled in his work? He will stand before kings; he will not stand before obscure men."

- To instill integrity and honor, my supervisor often reminded us that, "He who tends the fig tree will eat its fruit, and he who cares for his master will be honored" (Proverbs 27:18). I learned that honor is indeed a boomerang and what I displayed returned to me.

The workplace can be a big source of esteem and satisfaction, but Angela Duckworth quips, "Enthusiasm is common. Endurance is rare."[23] As we mature, we carve out a greater capacity to persevere and complete difficult projects. Duckworth adds, "One form of perseverance is the daily discipline of trying to do things better than we did yesterday... You must devote yourself to the sort of focused, full-hearted, challenge-exceeding-skill practice that leads to mastery."[24]

A compassionate thought to hold for others, as well as ourselves, is that we all are doing the best we can to become the people we are meant to be. It's easy to have blind spots at work, so let's consider ways to be gracious and thoughtful in our careers and ponder how we can make a kingdom impact. Here are ways to ensure you are making a gracious contribution at work.

Demonstrate Integrity

Think of time as a precious gift of honor that you offer to your employer and coworkers. I was brought up to believe that if you aren't five minutes early for work, you're late. Punctuality is key to honor and respect. Get to work on time, and don't leave early. Pay attention to your promptness around lunch and breaks too. You may think that your coworkers or boss don't notice, but they do!

A friend of mine complained that her coworker spent thirty minutes every morning and another thirty minutes every afternoon on social media! She worked an hour less per day than everyone else with this little trick. Though she thought she got away with it, it bred resentment among her peers.

Your company isn't paying you to be on Pinterest®, text with friends, or book personal appointments. Manage your time with integrity! Additionally, when you stay late or help with someone else's project, consider it a gift of honor and camaraderie you offer. Look for ways to come alongside a project to make a meaningful contribution. When we invest our time in someone else, the impact is significant.

Share Space Thoughtfully

Consider workspace an exercise in mindful graciousness. You are sharing space with other people. Are you mindful of how you impact that area?

I once had a coworker who parked his bike in front of the door. Everyone had to sidestep the muddy tires to enter. He would come to work, panting and sweaty from his bike ride, and throw his backpack on the floor of our shared cubicle. Then he would sit, giving the entire office a full view of his butt crack as he began making calls!

This guy's work was as good as anyone else's, but his habits were offensive. No one should have to smell you (or your lunch) when you enter the room, need to avert their eyes, or require noise-canceling earbuds to work alongside you. Be sensitive about your workspace. At minimum, make sure you don't burden anyone with your dishes, food, pets, or work materials. Practice graciousness through common courtesy.

Guard Your Words

Your words are the thermostat for your work environment. What you say sets the temperature, and this is true whether you are an entry-level employee or the boss. Remember, "The tongue of the wise brings healing" (Proverbs 12:18), and "A gentle answer turns away wrath, but a harsh word stirs up anger" (Proverbs 15:1). Your words can escalate tension or ease it. Consider how to build up rather than tear down, how to reward rather than criticize.

Leadership experts James Kouzes and Barry Posner of the Leavey School of Business at Santa Clara University, share some simple advice.

> *"Leaders recognize and reward what individuals do to contribute to vision and values. And they express their appreciation far beyond the limits of the organization's formal performance appraisal system. Leaders enjoy being spontaneous and creative in saying thank you, whether by sending notes, handing out personalized prizes, listening without interrupting, or trying any of a myriad number of other forms of recognition."*[25]

I'll never forget my first few years at Stanford University when all the campus religious groups would meet. A young gal from Menlo Park Presbyterian continually expressed gratitude for everyone's contribution. She did it in every meeting, and it struck me how that simple gesture of respect and appreciation shifted our atmosphere from competitive to friendly and cooperative.

Recently Andy and I were keynote speakers at a conference at the Museum of the Bible, alongside Mart Green, the Ministry Investment Officer for Hobby Lobby® and founder of Mardel® Christian stores. Green began his talk by recounting a central point from each of the seven previous speakers.

Did you get this picture? To begin his talk, the famous big-name speaker quoted each of the seven relatively unknown speakers. What an honor! Did it cost Green anything to do that? Nope, he simply modeled honor by paying attention, taking a few notes, and utilizing his words to bestow respect. Intentionally craft your words to release healing, peace, and appreciation into the workplace. Remember, your words are the thermostat for your work environment.

Obey the Law

We would think obeying the law is basic, right? But this is a tough call unless it's nailed down. Regardless of how lucrative it may be, how much pressure is exerted to comply, or the high stakes, don't do something illegal or dishonest.

The pressure to "bend the rules" or "fudge a bit" on numbers or dates, the desire to stack things in our favor, or cover our mistakes comes in subtle forms. You need a hard line that you will not participate, encourage, or tolerate anything illegal. Walk away from it; better yet, run!

Shun Discord

Gossip is probably everyone's top complaint about work politics. Yet, we all do it when we're stressed or hurt. People might not slam a coworker overtly, but they will slyly reveal that person's mistakes or annoying habits.

Don't trash-talk anyone you work with and always directly handle conflict. If you don't like what someone has done or said, speak with that person face to face to resolve the issue or consult your Human Resources department on how to proceed. Leadership experts say, "Humility is the only way to resolve the conflicts and contradictions of leadership. You can avoid excessive pride only if you recognize that you're human and need the help of others."[26]

The Apostle Paul tenderly urged Titus, "to malign no one, to be peaceable, gentle, showing every consideration for all men" (Titus 3:2). In our brash culture, this advice is a potent reminder that humility in the workplace is a vital aspect of gracious living!

Pray Continuously

Keep a running dialogue with God while you are at work. Scripture contains radical truth to shape your work experience. Verses such as Jeremiah 29:7, "Seek the welfare of the city where I have sent you into exile and pray to the Lord on its behalf; for in its welfare you will have welfare" give purpose to your prayers and work, which builds your commitment to labor for the good of your company.

Philippians 4:6-7 is a great motto that will shape a gracious attitude at work: "Be anxious for nothing, but in everything by prayer and supplication with thanksgiving let your requests be made known to God. And the peace of God, which surpasses all comprehension will guard your hearts and your minds in Christ Jesus."

The practice of prayer keeps you from worrying and fretting and guides you into a peaceful spot. The 1 Thessalonians

5:16-18 exhortation, "Rejoice always; pray without ceasing; in everything give thanks; for this is God's will for you in Christ Jesus" ushers in a peaceful, centered calm to everything you do. It's a reminder of the power of gratitude. If work is where you tend to separate your regular life from your spiritual life, bring an honest prayer dialogue with you to the office. Watch it transform your workday.

Google® pioneer Chade-Meng Tan teaches a ten-second exercise in thinking at work. He simply recommends identifying two people in the room and thinking, "I wish for this person to be happy, and I wish for that person to be happy."[27] Don't say anything else, just think it, Meng says. He calls this ten-second exercise the "joy of loving kindness" and promises it will increase your happiness too.

As Christ-followers, this is what we do all day long! We pray for God's blessing on our work, team, and company. We ask God for wisdom, kindness, joy, love, patience, excellence, endurance. We release these things over our employees and employers. When specific needs arise, we cover them in prayer, knowing that the Holy Spirit brings about change. Our prayers outweigh any wishful meditations. Prayer is your secret weapon for gracious behavior at work! Use it!

Organize as a Faith-based Community

Why stand alone as the only Christian at your job when you could band together and cultivate a godly culture? There is a "Faith and Work" movement sweeping across many industries these days.

Sue Warnke, a senior technology director for Salesforce in San Francisco, is also the president of Faithforce, an interfaith employee resource group. Founded in 2017, Faithforce has 2000 plus members in twelve regional hubs across five continents. There are Jesus-centered events in Silicon Valley that encourage all Christ-followers to gather for concerts, conferences, and prayer. In the summer with an influx of college interns, worship summer campfires are hosted at a beautiful park by the bay. Christian interns gather to network, worship, and eat smores. A faith community of career-oriented folks is a powerful force for gracious living.

Lead with Care

And now a bit of wisdom for the employer, manager, boss, head honcho—the Big Cheese. Scripture exhorts those in charge to, "Know well the condition of your flock and pay attention to your herds" (Proverbs 27:23).

Leaders are charged to know and understand those under their care because of the prominent role played.

> *"If you're a manager in an organization, to your direct reports you are the most important leader in your organization. You are more likely than any other leader to influence their desire to stay or leave, the trajectory of their careers, their ethical behavior, their ability to perform at their best, their drive to wow customers, their satisfaction with their jobs, and their motivation to share the organization's vision and values."*[28]

Leaders impact employees and coworkers. They should do it in a genuinely caring way, so that their actions advance the kingdom of God. Specifically, you can do three things:

• **Be a mentor.** My husband works in finance for one of the leading technology companies in Silicon Valley. He talks numbers all day long but, now and then, someone asks a personal question or seeks career advice. Andy says, "When someone asks, then it's an open door!" Asked about career, Andy unfolds his pattern of prayer and seeking God for direction. When asked about work-life balance, he opens up the concept of honor in the family and putting Christ first. He doesn't say things like, "You should do XYZ." Instead, he shares from a posture of personal experience by saying, "For me, it has been like XYZ."

Always be respectful with advice and aware of other cultural backgrounds. Andy has found that most younger staff value mentoring and career coaching. They invite feedback and appreciate development. Recently, he was able to encourage a discouraged young staffer that joy and a sense of self are not up for grabs. Andy told him, "No matter how things go at work, your joy and personal sense of self are yours alone to manage." With humility, Andy shared some of the mistakes he had made with boundaries and allowing his joy to be stolen by work. It was a transparent, vulnerable way to represent Christ to those watching at work. The young staffer appreciated the window into Andy's world, and Andy enjoyed speaking about a higher purpose.

- **Foster an environment of significance.** A work environment where significant relationships stand alongside accomplishment, commitment, and excellence is a great place to grow. My friend Kim worked at a low-priced shoe store in the mall. However, her commitment to that store was not low-end. One day, a man grabbed several boxes of shoes and dashed out of the store. Kim chased him through the parking lot until he threw down the boxes, jumped into his car, and yelled, "Stop chasing me!"

Although Kim's coworkers agreed it wasn't the smartest move, her fortitude strengthened store pride. The "Stop Chasing Me" jokes went on for months and even formed an identity of resilience and humor in her team. A mundane workplace morphed into a shining example of commitment and excellence.

If you ask employees for a big commitment, you will get a big commitment. And if you ask them for a small commitment, you will get precisely that. Foster an environment of significance and close-knit community, remembering, "Whatever you do, do your work heartily, as for the Lord rather than for men, knowing that from the Lord you will receive the reward of the inheritance. It is the Lord Christ whom you serve" (Colossians 3:23-24).

- **Engage the power of "thank you."** Words of acknowledgment from a godly employer go a long way in pointing someone to the goodness of God. And a sincere and personal "thank you" motivates employees more than you know. It's the language of a gracious employer.

Kouzes says, "There are few, if any, more basic needs than to be noticed, recognized, and appreciated for one's efforts. It's true for every one of us, whether we're volunteers, teachers, doctors, priests, politicians, salespeople, customer service representatives, maintenance staff, or executives. There's little wonder, then, that a greater volume of thanks is reported in highly innovative companies than in low-innovations firms."[29] Here's an example from leadership experts at Santa Clara University business school:

> *Aimee Blum experienced the power of "thank you" in her new company, much to her initial surprise. "If a client sends a compliment to a manager," she told us, "the manager will forward it to the entire company to let everyone know about a job well done." ...Aimee said that even in her short time with the company, she had received several*

*emails and positive comments about her perfor-
mance. "At first it surprised me. At my previous
company, compliments were rarely given; it was
expected that you would do a good job since you
were being paid to work there. But once I got used
to it, I found not only did I like receiving positive
feedback, I like giving it as well....Going from a
company that did not recognize contributions to
one that makes a point of it on a regular basis has
shown me how much of an impact simple gestures
can have on the work environment and how
they really instill a sense of community among
workers."*[30]

When Scripture labels people as fishermen or priests or tax collectors, it is acknowledging the human tendency to identify strongly with one's career. It's in the day-to-day rub of work that we extend grace, respect, and honor.

But aren't you glad Jesus was more than a carpenter? And you, my friend, must never forget that you are more than your career. You are more than a home builder, salesperson, financial analyst, writer, artist, nurse, housekeeper, surgeon, or teacher. Every day, you have the opportunity in your job to live and work graciously. Even more significant, you are a child of God, a blood-bought daughter of the King— accepted, forgiven, redeemed—filled with destiny and purpose! Bring your true identity into your career, and you will see your workplace transformed.

Meaningful Dialogue

1. How do you correlate your Christian beliefs at work with your thoughts, actions, and behaviors?

2. What is the atmosphere of your company? Who impacts it positively or negatively? How could you be the thermostat for your work atmosphere?

3. How is prayer incorporated into your work life?

4. How are you at receiving and expressing gratitude at work? What could you improve?

5. Do your coworkers know about your faith? Are there significant ways you can share who Christ is to you?

Declarations for Gracious Living

I am the light of the world! I bring wisdom, joy, and peace everywhere I go. (Matthew 5:14)

I do my work heartily as unto the Lord. (Colossians 3:23)

I give thanks for all things, for this is the will of God in Christ Jesus. (1 Thessalonians 5:18)

11

A Mentor's View

"Declaring the end from the beginning, And from ancient times things which have not been done."

ISAIAH 46:10A

Do you have the ability to see beyond someone's present behavior into the glorious destiny God has in mind? Such a clear vision, my friend, is the beautiful embodiment of grace and why I've included a chapter on mentoring in *Gracious Living*. Mentoring is a primary avenue for living graciously. The role of a mentor is to gift the truth of Isaiah 46:10 to another person—to help someone see the end from the beginning, to hold up the picture God holds of a blood-bought daughter as holy and beloved, destined for good works.

And that's what my mentor, Judy, did for me when I was a newbie Christian in high school. She was my Sunday school teacher, so she was happy to share the gospel. But she also embraced a dynamic role as she shared her life with me. I often ate dinners with her family and enjoyed Bible studies at her house. Judy became my spiritual mom as she fed my insatiable appetite for God with conferences, books, and daily quiet times. She reprimanded me, too, for things such as picking up hitchhikers, disrespecting my parents, and skinny-dipping at the lake!

Judy was continually holding up for me the picture of the woman God wanted me to become. When I didn't believe in myself, Judy believed for me. She always highlighted God's voice, and she turned my face toward Him, even on days when my neck was stubbornly stiff! Throughout my life, I've leaned on her clear-sighted vision of who I am meant to be. Her gift of Isaiah 46:10 rooted in my soul. And to this day, I keep on my desk a poem Judy gave me:

> "By looking at an acorn,
> Small and hard and plain,
> Could I conceive of oak trees?
> By listening to rain,
> Could I imagine oceans?
> Or could I understand
> The desert if my hand but held
> A single grain of sand?
> Then let me never think
> That what I chanced to see,
> This face, this frame, these thoughts,
> That this is all of me.
> Yet more than ageless oaks
> Or seas that have no shore,
> In me there also is
> Yet more, yet more.

-JAMES DILLET FREEMAN[31]

Getting to the More

In each of us, there is yet more. It's the *more* God planned, the more mentors can see, the diamond hiding in the rough coal. But most of us can't make that transformation based on a single hour each Sunday. We need mentors. We need those who know Jesus more than we do and care enough to walk beside us until we are safely and firmly secure in Christ. We need mentors who, along the way, dust off our skinned knees, point the way forward, celebrate our victories, and—now and then—thump our heads with eye-opening, behavior-altering truth that stings a bit but sticks!

The Apostle Paul exhorted the Corinthian church this way: "For if you were to have countless tutors in Christ, yet you would not have many fathers, for in Christ Jesus I became your father through the gospel" (1 Corinthians 4:15). We may follow multiple blogs and podcasts and sit under solid biblical teaching at church, but mentoring (being a spiritual mother or father) is a different level of closeness.

Paul was saying, "You might have many teachers in your faith, but there's a special place in your heart, and mine, for a spiritual father." Paul continued in verses 16-17, "Therefore, I exhort you, be imitators of me. For this reason, I have sent to you Timothy, who is my beloved and faithful child in the Lord, and he will remind you of my ways which are in Christ, just as I teach everywhere in every church."

Here's the modern-day translation of those verses: "You know me so well, imitate me, and because I want you to have a living example right in front of your eyes, I'm sending Timothy, my beloved child, to remind you of my ways. He talks like me, walks like me, and has my heart and mind in every situation." As Timothy's mentor, Paul led by example. Timothy followed Paul's lead and mentored others. And that's the way it should be in a gracious Christian community—the "I'll be there for you" promise passes from generation to generation.

Through example, affirmation, and dedication, spiritual mothers and fathers can graciously and lovingly mentor others into godly maturity. That's why Jesus mentored disciples, who then discipled the next generation of believers.

Think about the charge Jesus gave the eleven disciples after His resurrection: "Go therefore and make disciples of all the nations, baptizing them in the name of the Father and the Son and the Holy Spirit, teaching them to observe all that I commanded you" (Matthew 28:19-20). That charge remains with us today: *Go and make disciples.* We are not commanded to make converts nor churchgoers; we are instructed to make disciples, learners, Christ-followers. We are called to graciously and steadfastly mentor others.

Sharing the Treasure Map

Have you ever casually scanned a chapter in the Bible and instantly felt zinged by an indictment of your generation? I was reading 2 Kings 7 recently and came across the story of four lepers suffering in the time of famine. They concluded they would die where they were, so they might as well risk going to the enemy camp of the Arameans who might spare them.

As the lepers entered the enemy camp, they discovered empty tents and abandoned horses. Scriptures tells us, "When these lepers came to the outskirts of the camp, they entered one tent and ate and drank, and carried from there silver and gold and clothes, and went and hid them; and they returned and entered another tent and carried from there also, and went and hid them" (2 Kings 7:8). Reading this, I quickly sensed a summons in my spirit: *This is what the women in your generation have done, Margaret! They have eaten and drunk of My goodness and gathered treasures of Mine but have hidden them.*

Talk about a head thump! Whether through insecurity or selfishness, my generation of women has journeyed intimately with Christ but hidden those treasures. What a loss!

The four lepers in 2 Kings finally came to their senses. "We are not doing right. This day is a day of good news, but we are keeping silent ... let us go and tell" (2 Kings 7:9).

It's time for us to come to our senses too. I believe a movement is rising for mature women to invest in younger generations and to mentor these women into spiritual maturity. It's time for us to go and tell!

We possess a treasure map leading to riches in Christ, and we must share it. How do we do this? To begin, we need identities of fullness and possession. We must believe we have something to give away! By overcoming the hurdles of scarcity thinking, we can run toward the rich prize of mentoring a new generation of leaders.

So, ask yourself a few questions.

- Do you meet Christ consistently in a daily quiet time? Whether you've lingered in His presence for two years or twenty, think how to demonstrate that discipline to a younger woman.

- Do you know how to encourage your husband and children in the Lord? Retrace your steps in gaining that priority and share it with younger wives.

- Have you overcome addictions and negative self-talk? Translate that process to younger gals who are longing to find their way through the darkness.

You own a unique treasure map to riches in Christ. Share it!

The Heart of the Matter

Understanding the depth and beauty of the treasure you have to share is one wing of a bird, but for the bird to fly, it needs another wing: a heart for your mentee.

When the Apostle Paul was concerned for the Philippian church, he sent Timothy with this explanation: "For I have no one else of kindred spirit who will genuinely be concerned for your welfare. For they all seek after their own interests, not those of Christ Jesus" (Philippians 2:20-21). Of all the young men Paul discipled and trained, he only commended Timothy as "genuinely concerned for your welfare."

Focus on those words, "only Timothy." In your circle of faith friends is there widespread genuine concern for younger women? Or, do only one or two women have a heart for mentoring?

Such a small number of mentors is another head thump for mature women of faith. You see, we can absorb all kinds of riches in Christ, but until we engage a genuine, heartfelt concern for a mentee, the treasure remains ours alone.

Heartfelt concern should stand as a guide rail for both the mentor and the mentee: find someone who genuinely cares for you. No one wants to be somebody's project! We do all, however, long for genuine relationships. A spiritual mother will pursue a deep understanding of her mentee. Looking each other in the eye with great love and understanding is a gracious gift offered to both the mentor and mentee. Conversely, wounds and discouragement arise from not valuing each other deeply.

In all honesty, I've tried mentoring a few young people based on their need more than a calling to help them. In a lapse of judgment, I forgot the saying that a need does not constitute a call. In these instances, my efforts fell flat. Somehow, they could sense the routineness of it and my lack of heart commitment. Mentoring, merely as a rote program, will never aspire to the life-changing impact of a true spiritual mother. Mentoring with a sincere heart for your mentee will anchor your focus on God's promises rather than current problems. Then, an honoring and gracious relationship will blossom.

A gal I mentored at Stanford came to me heartbroken and discouraged. She had hooked up with a guy whom she cared nothing about. She felt out of control and discouraged that her faith hadn't prevented her risky behavior. As we talked, God graciously gave me a picture of her in the future as a godly, joyous woman. Confidently I could declare over her, "Hooking up is not who you are and not where you're headed."

We were able to engage her hopefulness and desire to be all that God had designed her to be. Through mutual tears, we severed any partnership with shame, discouragement, or seeking comfort outside of God's boundaries. Following the Holy Spirit's leading brought me to the exact ingredient needed to bring insight and change in her life. God was not fretting in heaven over that gal's mistakes! He was not wringing His hands, saying, *Oh no, what am I going to do with this one!* Instead, God placed this girl in my heart, and the Holy Spirit showed me how to take her by the hand to see the end from the beginning, to hold up the picture God holds of a blood-bought daughter as holy and beloved, destined for good works.

Sure, at times, we have to get down and dirty with the details of how a mentee is living it out. However, we must always maintain a firm grasp and steely-eyed vision on her future. We walk a tightrope between unconditional acceptance and straight-edge coaching. But it is God who is at work to will and to do for His good pleasure. He is working. When you take three steps back, when you relapse, when you fail, God is still working.

Making the Connection

In her article, "Generational Mentorship: What Millennial Mentees Want," Erin Seheult summed up what this generation hungers for: "Millennials want mentors who communicate, participate, demonstrate, and validate. More than any other generation in the work force, millennials desire mentors."[32]

Do you ever notice an interest in a younger woman for a mentoring relationship? If so, how do you make the connection? Although, for some, it is an instantaneous decision, for most, the process involves gradually increasing the relationship.

First, I get clarity on what I have to offer. I gather and organize the tools I've acquired over the years. Then, I bring my life alongside women who want mentors. That means I have to get out there and relate to more than just women my age and life stage. I start putting people on my prayer list and see if God reveals insights for me to share. Does a particular woman or group of gals stand out to me? Do I keep finding them on my heart and mind? If yes, then I keep praying for them, maybe initiate some texts or emails or reach out to grab coffee.

As I see a desire to grow in the person, opportunities to answer questions come up, and I offer encouragement and affirmation. I pray for God to give me dreams and insights for my mentees, as well as special grace and affection for them. More than meeting once a week for an hour over coffee, we share our lives. If I am speaking somewhere, I invite them along. If they are leading or speaking somewhere, I go along. They see how I respond to traffic, salesclerks, laundry machines breaking, and bills needing payment. And I see how they process these things as well.

Anyone can talk a good game for an hour over coffee. But I need to walk alongside my mentees throughout everyday experiences to offer real insight into their lives. I need to see how they treat their children, husbands, friends, and acquaintances. Without this close-up view, I only know what they tell me, and blind spots remain. When a clear picture is seen, I must walk the tightrope between unconditional acceptance and coaching.

Your church may already operate in a mentoring culture. Intentional leaders may have already developed a norm of mentoring and discipling every new person who comes through the door. Or, it may be up to you to initiate such a culture. All it takes is a few believers who value the treasure that results from one-on-one mentoring relationships.

One summer, my son, Cooper, and I were setting goals. He mentioned some things he was struggling with, namely being close to God. Cooper concluded that he needed a mentor. One of the youth leaders stood out to Cooper as a guy he could follow and learn from.

We discussed how he would go about it. Here's what I told him: Don't ask somebody to mentor you. It's too much pressure. Instead, text him to meet for coffee or a hike or whatever. Tell him you have a few questions to ask. Go with the quest to get to know this guy and for him to get to know you. Afterward, think about how it went. Did he give you solid insight on your questions? Do you respect him? Does he seem to understand you? Follow that pattern a few more times. If you are sensing benefit and a deepening relationship, set up a regular meeting time with something like this: "Hey, I feel like I'm growing as a believer because of our discussions and prayer together. Can we set up a regular time each week to go over what I'm thinking about and for you to bring things you think I should be thinking about?" If you feel good about it after a month or so, I would say you have a mentor!

This is common sense. But many of us try to rush the process or set up an unnatural type of hierarchy that ends up feeling awkward. Sure, you can have many people who serve as coaches in specific areas of your walk with God. But as Paul said, you may have many tutors, but only one spiritual mother or father. The process of growing into that type of a lifelong relationship takes time. Choose wisely and go slowly!

Good Questions

Because gracious mentoring serves a precise function and is underutilized in many faith communities, I want to answer some questions to help us wrap our arms around it. These questions often arise when someone is considering a mentoring relationship as a spiritual mother or father.

Q: Do we have to meet every week?

A: There's no "one size fits all" in mentoring. Some people need a lot of encouragement and education. For example, someone just coming out of an addictive lifestyle might need to talk to her mentor daily. A new Christian will probably need consistency more than anything else. Do what is healthy and beneficial for both of you. Several texts a week are simple ways to feel connected and share insights. Utilizing connections already in place, like social media, strengthens the bonds between you.

Q: Do we need to go through a mentoring book or study?

A: Utilizing material is helpful. The mentoring journey runs smoother if you have an idea of where you're headed. It's easy to get in a rut of staring at each other blankly and rehashing the same things every week. Study a book of the Bible together, or go through a course on prayer or parenting or whatever is relevant to your mentee. Put solid biblical teaching in front of her eyes and ears regularly. Survey often to uncover areas of growth or confusion.

To save you a lot of research time, here's a list of my favorite mentoring resources:

- *The Lost Art of Disciple Making* by LeRoy Eims (Zondervan). The list of thirty mentor training objectives is an especially helpful tool.

- *The Purple Book: Biblical Foundations for Building Strong Disciples* by Rice Broocks and Steve Murrell (Zondervan) I typically go through this twelve-week study with new believers. It helps ensure we have all the basics covered. It becomes a tool my mentees can employ in mentoring others.

- *The God I Never Knew: How Real Friendship with the Holy Spirit can Change Your Life* and *The Blessed Life: Unlocking the Rewards of Generous Living* by Robert Morris (Gateway Create Publishing). Both books are linear, biblical, and easy to read and discuss. They will revolutionize your understanding of the Holy Spirit and inspire your generosity.

- *The Bait of Satan* by John Bevere (Charisma House). This book shaped my expression of faith and forgiveness. I consider it foundational for any new believer.

- *Desperate: Hope for the Mom Who Needs to Breathe* by Sarah Mae and Sally Clarkson (Thomas Nelson Publishers). This book is a delightful breath of fresh air for an exhausted mom.

- *The Secret Thoughts of an Unlikely Convert* by Rosaria Champagne Butterfield (Crown and Covenant). This is a deeply thoughtful and provocative read for anyone strug gling with same-sex attractions.

Other favorite authors include C.S. Lewis, Catherine Marshall, and Bill Johnson. These thought leaders should keep you and your mentee sourced with input for a long time. As you and your mentee progress, keep a core value of curiosity rather than control regarding resources. Don't only study from one camp within Christianity. Be curious about how evangelicals share their faith versus Pentecostals. Unfortunately, this curiosity is not reflected in denominational bookstores, so search online! If you both aren't big readers, find favorite podcasts to listen to and discuss.

Q: Does a mentor introduce topics other than spirituality and Bible study?

A: Anything that increases someone's effectiveness in the kingdom of God is fair game. Think about all the ways we don't connect the dots: how being late and not managing our time dishonors people, how maintaining an orderly peaceful home makes others feel at peace, or how ignorance in budgeting can hurt one's family life. All of these and a multitude of little life choices nuance our effectiveness for Christ. These are the topics that may not make it to the top thirty list of things you need to teach your mentee, but they bubble up to the surface when there is confusion.

For example, my friend, Jamil, mentors a college freshman. They met at the gym several times a week to work out, but the kid was always late. One day after a workout, Jamil spent two hours training him in calendaring and time management. When Jamil met the young man's parents months later, they didn't talk about their son's new theology; they talked about how he was always on time now and making better grades in school! A mentor with a careful eye and a listening spirit will discern what areas of growth the mentee needs to prosper in body, soul, and spirit.

Q: What are some pitfalls to avoid in mentoring?

A: Most mentoring mistakes relate to either wandering or controlling. I'm a wanderer. Studying discipleship material keeps me on course. Keeping the focus is important. I may become close to a mentee, but I remind myself she has plenty of friends but only one mentor. The controllers get overzealous and take responsibility for their mentee's success, but we're not the Junior Holy Spirit! We cannot convict another person of sin, nor reveal to them what God is saying in their life. A mentee's abdication of control reveals an unhealthy, unbalanced relationship. The mentee should possess freedom of choice in a non-judgmental environment.

The biggest pitfall of all is never mentoring, never investing in someone else's journey. Rudyard Kipling said, "Gardens are not made by singing, 'Oh how beautiful,' and sitting in the shade."[33] We can admire the idea of mentoring, or we can fear the possibilities. Neither matter, however, if we don't get out there and try it. Don't get caught up in doing it perfectly that you never do anything! Truly gracious believers invest as best they can in the next generation.

Your job as a gracious mentor is to hold up a mirror for your mentee to see her true beauty. Be her champion! Remind her often of God's value for her and the destiny He has planned. Benjamin Disraeli, who twice served as the Prime Minister of the United Kingdom, reportedly once said, "The greatest good you can do for another is not just share your riches but to reveal to him his own."[34] Brag about your mentee and don't be stingy with your honor and affection.

The Apostle Paul, when writing to the believers in Thessalonica, said, "For we proved to be gentle among you, as a nursing mother tenderly cares for her own children. Having so fond an affection for you, we were well-pleased to impart to you not only the gospel of God but also our own lives, because you had become very dear to us" (1 Thessalonians 2:7-8). Stop and think for a moment about Paul's analogy. Although he lived in a male-dominated society, the apostle described a nursing mother to drive home a point: As tenderly and thoughtfully as a mother cares for an infant, that is the posture of a mentor.

Paul added that he was pleased to not only share information about Christ but to give away his own life in the process. I know someone like that.

Jamil, a 23-year-old campus minister, heard about Mikey long before he ever met him. Mikey was the number one party-guy at the college. Every student in the party scene sought Mikey out for the lowdown on the next weekend's events.

Mikey usually cruised campus with a beautiful girl on his arm, but one day, Jamil noticed him sitting alone. Instantly Jamil sensed the Holy Spirit saying, *Go talk to Mikey. Tell him about My love.*

Jamil reveled in God's power to change anyone's life, even Mikey's. As they spoke earnestly, Mikey said, "I want to reach God, Jamil, but I've done too much bad." With a cigarette tucked behind his ear, Mikey began to weep. Jamil prayed with him to be born again.

That same night, Mikey and Jamil joined a Bible study in the dorm. They met almost every day that week as major transformation exploded in Mikey's life. Jamil graciously visited Mikey's apartment to help him throw away his bongs and drug paraphernalia.

Jamil also invited Mikey to share the gospel on campus with him the following week. One student Jamil approached kept looking distractedly at Mikey until finally, he blurted, "Hey man, weren't you at the party two weeks ago?" Mikey replied with conviction, "Yeah, man, but I'm not about that anymore. You wake up the next morning, and everything you wanted from that party still isn't there. I've finally found peace, and it's because of Jesus." Mikey, a two-week-old Christian, led that student to Christ, with Jamil's help, began to mentor him.

Jamil reflected recently, "Big fruit doesn't transpire in one year; it's ten years later seeing Mikey thriving as a successful husband, father, and business owner.

Jamil just turned thirty-five and has mentored over fifty young students. Those fifty have led many others to Christ, and yes, they are mentoring them and sharing their lives to bring others to fulness in Christ. Jamil is building the kingdom through multiplication!

Begin speaking the truth of Isaiah 46:10 to others. Help them see the end from the beginning. Hold up the picture God holds of a blood-bought daughter or son as holy and beloved, destined for good works. This picture, my friend, is the apex of a gracious life.

Meaningful Dialogue

1. Explore the ways Jesus mentored His disciples. How could you use His methods in your life?

2. Have you been mentored at church or work? Have you ever been a mentor for someone else? Describe your experiences.

3. What do you consider obstacles to mentorship? Do you have any concerns about time, relationships, or Bible knowledge?

4. How can you keep your guidance positive and free from judgment?

5. Is there someone God deposited on your heart to mentor? Pray about this now!

Declarations for Gracious Living

I have discovered treasures in Christ, and I will not hide them! (Colossians 2:3)

"Now we who are strong ought to bear the weaknesses of those without strength and not just please ourselves." (Romans 15:1)

I imitate God as a beloved child. I walk in love just as Christ loved. (Ephesians 5:1)

12

Stranger Things

"For I was hungry, and you gave Me something to eat;
I was thirsty, and you gave Me something to drink;
I was a stranger, and you invited Me in."
MATTHEW 25:35

I was sipping coffee with my friend Joanne when she excitedly said, "God is so good, Margaret! Right before I came over, a telemarketer called on my home phone and gave me his pitch. I told him we weren't remodeling anytime soon, and then asked, 'Do you need prayer for anything?' He said he had an argument with his wife before he left the house, and so his day hadn't been that great. I prayed that God would put forgiveness in both their hearts, reconcile them and that they would once again have their first love for each another. He said, 'Wow! Thank you so much. I appreciate that!' Margaret, it was such a sweet interaction, and he was genuinely touched! I'm just so thankful I was home to answer his call!"

Now before you sink into guilt about your last interaction with a marketer, here's a gentle reminder: we're all on a journey. We grow toward gracious living, and we have different gifts and varying moods from day to day. Joanne is susceptible to self-centered living, just like the rest of us, but she has invested lots of time and personal work modeling graciousness toward anyone and everyone.

If my conversation with Joanne were a one-time anomaly, I would think *Wow! That's nice but slightly weird.* However, Joanne probably has a conversation like this every few days. It's how she rolls! My gracious friend has prayed for a young telemarketer's terminally ill aunt, along with a salesman whose daughter had a brain tumor. Joanne has shared the gospel and prayed with enough telemarketers dialing from a call center in India that her name is probably known there. Joanne laughingly concludes, "I'm advancing the kingdom of God one telemarketer at a time!"

Hmmm, I must confess that where telemarketers are concerned, sometimes a switch flips in my brain: *I don't want to have to be kind to "those people!"* Who is it for you? Is it salespeople? Illegal immigrants? Other drivers on the freeway? How about the homeless man at the intersection? Or just any stranger? Being gracious toward strangers takes some practice, no small amount of patience, and some God chat.

Bringing Heaven to Earth

Author Henry Blackaby once said, "God clearly spoke to His people in Acts. He clearly speaks to us today. From Acts to the present, God has been speaking to His people by the Holy Spirit. Because He is always present in a believer, He can speak to you clearly at any time and in any way He chooses."[35]

Joanne constantly asks God to speak to her about the people she encounters in Target, at the grocery store, gas station, and so on. Here's no surprise: Joanne has prayed for people in every place imaginable, all because she asks God to show her where He's at work around her.

Just so you know, Joanne is not loud, boisterous, or even someone you would describe as outgoing. She simply asks God what He thinks and obeys whatever He says to do. Once, when she was in the school carpool line, she noticed a Ford F150 parked in front of her with the bass thumping loudly. Joanne felt God's nudging, "Go talk with the man in that truck." Joanne had to first work through some mental gymnastics: *Is that really You, God? What should I say?* She felt God's answer, *He needs an encounter with My love!*

Joanne will tell you that her natural self would never do such a thing, but her born-again redeemed spirit, partnering with the Holy Spirit, got the message! She climbed out of her car, not knowing what she was going to say, and walked up to his window to introduce herself. Then she felt led to ask, "Do you have pain in your body?" The man replied that he was a construction worker and had pain all the time, especially in his back. Joanne asked if she could pray for him, and then prayed that he would know how much God loves him, sees him, and wants him well. It was a quick prayer because the students were pouring out of their classes, but the man teared up and acknowledged God's healing touch on his body. To Joanne, it was one more seed of God's love sown in the world, one more experience of bringing heaven to earth.

Poet Edgar Guest wrote, "There are no strangers here; only friends you haven't yet met."[36] That pretty much sums up life for me. I enjoy chatting with just about anyone! Recently, I flew to Los Angeles to help my daughter, Brooke, move out of her dorm at USC. At Alamo, I felt God prompt me to share with the car rental gal, Whitney, a dream I recently had. "Do you believe God speaks through dreams?" I asked. "Yes, I do," she answered. Then, the woman working next to her interrupted us to say, "I'm sorry to butt in—and she spilled a story about her sister warning her through a dream. She ignored the warning and had an accident. The three of us encouraged one another with the ways God had been speaking to us. This was not your usual mundane car rental interaction!

As I headed out to the lot, I asked the Alamo staffer, Ahmet, "Which is the fastest car?" Laughing, I told him, "I'm used to driving a fast car, and I want something that will keep up!" We were joking around about our driving habits, and I sensed God reminding me of a Scripture I had just read about purpose. I shared the word with Ahmet and said a blessing over his life. Then I raced off in a Chevy Malibu to pick Brooke up at the dorm.

The minute she saw my car, Brooke said, "Mom, there's no way my stuff will fit in that!" So, we had to go right back to Alamo. Brooke and I walked in just as Whitney was about to take a break. She strode over to me, past a line of people, and acted as if we were long lost cousins. Whitney gave me the VIP treatment on getting a bigger car at no cost. Out we went to the lot, and who do you think came running up to greet us? Ahmet, waving enthusiastically, was calling my name. As I drove away in a Suburban, Brooke, absolutely baffled, asked, "How do all these people know you, Mom?" Grinning, I answered, "I just bring heaven to earth, baby girl! Heaven to earth."

The Warmth of Vulnerability

It's so much fun to walk with God, listening to His voice! If we tune in to Him, the Holy Spirit guides, warns, protects, and inspires us. There are no strangers, just friends you haven't yet met when you listen to God's guidance on whom to talk to and whom to avoid.

Can it be we're still living under the fear campaign that ran in the 1960s that coined the phrase "stranger danger"? It received criticism for confusing kids into believing that everyone they know is safe and anyone you don't know is unsafe. We need to use our intuition and good sense and listen to God's promptings to walk wisely and obediently to the call of Christ. I don't appreciate memorized, canned approaches to people. But if we will listen to the Holy Spirit, He will give us fresh, insightful ways to care for the people around us. He makes even a mundane trip to Alamo an adventure!

Why is graciousness toward strangers so intertwined in Christian Scriptures, as well as almost every dominant religion? Exodus 23:9 sheds some light: "You shall not oppress a stranger, since you yourselves know the feelings of a stranger, for you also were strangers in the land of Egypt."

That fundamental understanding of graciousness holds in every culture. At some point, we all are vulnerable, lost, or alone in a new place—and we sure appreciate someone reaching out! God even declares, "Then I will draw near to you for judgment; and I will be a swift witness against the sorcerers and against the adulterers and against those who swear falsely, and against those who oppress the wage earner in his wages, the widow and the orphan, and those who turn aside the alien and do not fear Me," says the LORD of hosts" (Malachi 3:5).

God is not cool with rudeness to strangers, my friend! He's the God who cares for the widow and orphan, the stranger, and the oppressed, and He expects us to do the same! Vulnerability is a common ingredient for widows, orphans, and strangers. It heightens every new experience, whether it's being new to a classroom, a neighborhood, or a country. Being vulnerable and a stranger is part of the human experience, so of course, God cares.

One of the most gracious families I've ever known welcomed us into our new neighborhood in 2010. Kol Church quickly raised his hand when my son's third-grade teacher asked the class, "Who wants to welcome our new student and show him around the classroom?" Kol and Cooper were instant friends.

The apple didn't fall far from that tree, because Kol's mom is the same way. All it took was one afternoon at pickup for Anh-Dao to introduce me to all the moms in the neighborhood. Anh-Dao is an athletic bundle of friendly. She's the women's tennis coach at San Jose State University and seems to know everyone in town. I once asked her why she is so welcoming and her quick reply was, "I'm going to be friendly and reach out because that's what I want the world to be!"

It turns out that Anh-Dao has quite a story. It began with the fall of Saigon, which ended the Vietnam war in April of 1975. At age 13, Anh-Dao, along with her parents and five siblings, secretly boarded a boat headed for the United States. They landed in a refugee center that had sprung up at Camp Pendleton in San Diego to help with the exodus of over 100,000 Vietnamese. Anh-Dao's father had been a colonel in the army. Even though he was from an honored and wealthy family, they had to leave it all behind and begin anew.

Vietnamese refugees were required to have a sponsor in the states to exit the refugee camp. The Sutton family—a mom, dad, sixteen-year-old girl, twelve-year-old sister, and a five-year-old brother—lived in Albertville, Alabama, and learned of Anh-Dao's family through their church outreach. When the Suttons thought about those six kids, ages two to fifteen, living in a refugee camp, they decided to become Anh-Dao's family sponsor. They took them into their home and shared meals and daily life, even though no one in Anh-Dao's family spoke English.

Can you imagine having a family of eight crowded into your house? Sandi Sutton was sixteen when Anh-Dao's family moved into her home. She helped drive them to doctor's appointments, grocery stores, and English classes. Anh-Dao's family was deeply appreciative of the Suttons, and the Suttons learned thankfulness from their Vietnamese family. When Sandi left to attend college, she vividly remembered Anh-Dao's father standing in their driveway for the goodbye with tears streaming down his cheeks. Anh-Dao remains an ardent Alabama Crimson Tide fan and is forever grateful for the Sutton family welcoming her to our country.

Little Keys to Big Doors

Kindness toward strangers doesn't have to be a considerable commitment. Recently, I watched my chiropractor take a phone call when his assistant was busy helping other clients. He didn't realize I was watching as the call turned out to be an inquiry about another chiro office. He patiently answered questions and even looked up the address for them! You see, he decided a long time ago that graciousness is a part of his fabric. It doesn't matter if he feels like it or if it's convenient.

"It is little keys that open up big doors," said poet Lamine Pearlheart.[37] Watching my chiropractor field that phone call reminded me he's a safe and sage man. I trust him because kindness is an integral part of his being.

If kindness and gracious words and actions toward strangers are the little keys, what big doors do they open?

• **The door to our culture.** Gracious living shapes our culture. We are the ones to bring heaven to earth. We are the ones to establish the culture under the King's reign, and it's not short-tempered! We create beauty, gentleness, and compassion through our gracious words and actions. Imagine if every Christian in the United States acted like my friend Joanne, prayerfully searching for opportunities throughout the day? Or the Sutton family, reaching out to those in need of a haven?

• **The door to the gospel.** Kindness toward strangers releases a convergence of modern living with the gospel. We represent Christ in all His goodness in humble and straightforward acts of offering hospitality to strangers. We live out the gospel in modern ways every time we extend kindness to strangers and those in need. Who else is going to share the gospel in that call center in India? How about in Target or the grocery store?

• **The door to our destiny.** Graciousness extended to strangers fulfills our destiny. We all feel it—that sense of being made for more than what we are living. We know we could do better and live larger than we do. When we sever ties to self-focused living, we unlock a big door called our future. Scan the list of your closest friends and see if you didn't meet through kindness or graciousness proffered.

Fully Known

One of the hardest places to land is the feeling that God is a stranger. "Hear my prayer, O Lord, and give ear to my cry; Do not be silent at my tears; for I am a stranger with You, a sojourner like all my fathers" (Psalms 39:12). Have you ever experienced this kind of anguish—as if you were a stranger to God, and He to you? You can cry out to God, and yet He feels so far away.

Times like these can transform our lives and choices, entangling us with confusion, lies, and doubt. But as the psalmist wrote, "Only the rebellious dwell in a parched land. God makes a home for the lonely; He leads out the prisoners into prosperity" (Psalm 68:6). We may feel lost and estranged at times, but thankfully our God is unfailing. He hasn't forgotten us. He's 100 percent committed to finding us and releasing our hearts to know Him and be fully understood.

That's what God did for a young guy who came to my house to deliver a bike. He and a coworker unloaded it and needed about twenty minutes to set it up and connect it online. I asked if they wanted something to drink—water or because it was a chilly morning, hot tea. One of the young men perked up and said, "I'd love a cup of tea." He had just moved to the coast from Arizona and was cold all the time in our Northern Cal weather.

When I went into the kitchen to make his tea, I reached for a mug but distinctly felt I should give him one off the top shelf. I grabbed it and made the tea. The mug had printed on it, "God will always give me the victory." I turned it so the words faced him, and said, "This is a true word for you today, my friend, God will always give you the victory. I don't know what you're going through, but you're going to come out on the right side of it."

The young man just stared at me for an awkward ten seconds. Then he shook his head in amazement. I was starting to feel that maybe I had messed up and perhaps offended him. But he let out a big sigh and said that he'd just moved to California after finishing a career in sports. He was trying to get his life together with a fresh start. He was wondering, even that morning, if God knew where he was. We talked openly for about five minutes, and then I prayed a blessing over his life and plans. We had both shown up to get a bike installed and then move on to the next thing. Yet, something significant and unique happened in that space.

I almost always feel that beautiful things happen when we are mindful and listen to the Holy Spirit's guidance about the people around us. Being gracious toward strangers is, first and foremost, about honoring the person in front of you.

When I reflect on the kind of person I hope to become and the type of city I want to live in, I can quickly feel overwhelmed. How can I make a difference in the world when I struggle even to make changes in myself? The answer is baby steps—little keys opening big doors. Or, as Jesus put it, "It is like leaven, which a woman took and hid in three pecks of flour until it was all leavened" (Luke 13:21).

God has hidden His leaven, the Holy Spirit, in us. Like my friend Anh-Dao, we can welcome strangers, not only because that's what God did for us, but also because we are creating the world in which we want to live. Through the Holy Spirit's empowerment, we throw open our lives to welcome strangers from other countries and here at home while we're shopping at Target, getting gas, and yes, even answering those phone calls from telemarketers.

Meaningful Dialogue

1. What are small and large gestures of kindness you can show to strangers? Do you have any recent examples?

2. How have strangers shown grace or kindness to you? How did that feel?

3. How can you adopt a lifestyle of actively looking to bless others as you go about your day?

4. Do spiritual conversations come up in your interactions? How do you transition from chit-chat to something of depth?

Declarations for Gracious Living

I trust in the Lord in all my ways, and I don't lean on my understanding. (Proverbs 3:5)

God is always speaking. I partner with Him to release truth, grace, and beauty. (1 Peter 4:11)

I am enthusiastic about doing good works. (1 Peter 3:13)

God created me for good works which He has already prepared for me to do. (Ephesians 2:10)

13

Social Media Reclaim

"Let the words of my mouth and the meditation
of my heart be acceptable in your sight,
O Lord, my Rock and my Redeemer."

PSALMS 19:14

As a child growing up in Houston, I loved to hang out at a playground near my home. A tall fort stood as the centerpiece among the play structures. It featured a shiny metal slide that blazed butt-scorching hot in the summer. My friends and I would spend hours at the structure after school.

But one summer, a gang of aggressive older boys seized the fort as their exclusive territory. Several feeble attempts made by me and my friends to invoke sharing unleashed a barrage of soda cans and swear words from the fort's peak. We tried to stage a coup one day, arriving early and draping blankets from the roof to establish our claim. I still remember the sounds of their Schwinn bikes crunching the gravel path and their tennis shoes banging up the metal slide to tear down our blankets and send us packing. The fort was no longer fun—or safe.

Fifty years later, I'm in a similar predicament with social media. Facebook® launched in 2004, and I jumped on board in 2009. At first, I slurped up news as I reconnected with college roommates and high-school friends I hadn't seen in twenty years. Through Facebook, I also linked with women I regularly saw at church, work, and school as I shared in all kinds of personal events they posted. Their Pinterest pictures of home projects introduced new inspirations and a sense of connectedness.

Yes, the early days of social media were holistic and beneficial. My friend, Pamela, was moving to a new city for her first job after college. As she pulled into town, all her possessions stuffed into her Subaru hatchback, she got a phone call; her housing situation had fallen through at the last minute. What did Pamela do? She walked into the nearest Starbucks and posted her dilemma on her social media sites. Within minutes, words of encouragement, along with suggestions for accommodations, started rolling in. Through a friend of a friend on Facebook, Pamela found lodging at an auntie's house for several weeks before moving into an apartment. Social media also connected her with a church and a gym. Multiple comments of "You got this!" and "Hey, praying for you, girl!" flooded her feed for days. This spirit is what we all long for in our online communities: acknowledgment, information, support, and encouragement.

However, in the last few years, bit by bit, post by post, an aggressive invasion has begun to dominate social media. But unlike the bullies who seized my childhood fort, we've invaded social media from within, slowly tossing down our warm blankets of connectivity and replacing them with negativity, comparison, and overconsumption. What began as a fun playground is now entangled with spiteful barbs, arguing, comparison, posturing, and denigration. It gravitates toward an "us versus them" mindset of political rhetoric and shallow reposting. Sadly, social media has become butt-scorching hot. The culture is no longer fun, and perhaps not even safe.

So, what can we do about that? How can we graciously reclaim social media?

Acknowledge the Source

Almost any moment of any day, you can find an online rant against people, places, foods, behaviors, and organizations. We release into the cyber community our denunciation of everything from cats to the Catholic church, our opinions forming a cacophony of nihilism. How many butt-searing angry rants can you read online before your emotions are scorched?

Political posts are some of the most incendiary. In 2009, several of my Facebook friends posted some version of "Obama is the anti-Christ." These days, I see others posting, "Trump is the anti-Christ" and "Not My President." I'm thankful I see both sides embody my social media, and I worry for folks who don't have that representation in their "friends" group. However, when was the last time you read a thoughtful, reflective, personal essay on someone's political or religious views? Can't remember? Me neither. It's too easy to repost a political or religious article that echoes our opinion rather than formulating well-reasoned personal thoughts. Some friends that I characterize as loving, godly people are somehow comfortable posting hateful, thoughtless attacks on social media. The trashy flood of unrestrained posts and reposts is wearying. The efforts to incite hatred are increasingly evident. Polarizing sensational click-bait floods my online experience.

So, what's the salve for all the acidic rhetoric? Well, first we must acknowledge its source so we can guard against it and create a gracious alternative. Ironically, words the Apostle Paul posted in the first century get to the heart of twenty-first century social-media venom:

> *"For men will be lovers of self, lovers of money, boastful, arrogant, revilers, disobedient to parents, ungrateful, unholy, unloving, irreconcilable, malicious gossips, without self-control, brutal, haters of good, treacherous, reckless, conceited, lovers of pleasure rather than lovers of God, holding to a form of godliness, although they have denied its power. Avoid such men as these." (2 Timothy 3:2-5)*

Negativity and bashing aren't new events in the world; they're showcased in a new form. Every description the Apostle Paul penned in 2 Timothy 3:2-5 could reflect the average social media feed. Don't believe me? Well, let's take a look.

- Do you see lovers of self? (Show me your selfie stick.)
- How about haters of good? (Let's spew anger and divide people.)
- Reckless discussion? (Haven't we all boarded an escalating comment stream?)
- Malicious gossips? (Entire industries are dedicated to that.)

The Apostle Paul's advice for purging this negativity is direct: avoid such people. And I'll add this purging counsel: don't be that person. Some people love to stir the pot, but you and I can choose not to jump into the swirling cesspool!

Proverbs 6:27 asks this question: "Can a man take fire in his bosom and his clothes not be burned?" In other words, can you and I merely warm ourselves by the fire of online negativity, anger, and accusation without being burned? Perhaps, but surely, we'll smell like smoke from that campfire!

Is avoidance the only answer? *No.* Every click warrants evaluation and self-discipline. We must ask ourselves *How does this website, TV show, blog, post, or picture impact my thinking? Does it usher in positive, hopeful, informative thoughts? Or does it introduce negativity, discord, and superficial or destructive ideas?* Most click-bait is effective because our hearts gravitate toward contention. The more sensational the content, the more we are drawn to it! We steward our spiritual and emotional health by monitoring our online intake with keen eyes. Reclaiming the positivity of social media begins with each of us—and every click.

Resist the Dare to Compare

Maybe your social media experience isn't jarred by discord and people-bashing. Perhaps all you see are beautifully photographed vacations or wedding portraits, romantic dinners, and sunsets. Maybe you witness a steady stream of crazy-cool ski videos and GoPro footage of cliff jumping into deep-blue pools.

Recently, I enjoyed a beautiful holiday in Southern France, but when I saw a friend post from a sunny spot in Italy, I felt a twinge of comparison: *Does her sky look bluer than mine? Look how thin she is!* Pathetic, right? But many of us struggle with that competitive, comparative problem of jealousy.

In Karen Ehman's study, "What Matters Most," ninety-eight percent of her social media followers struggled to look at the social media accounts of others without feeling a bit of jealousy, which led to discontent. What areas amplified that jealousy? According to Ehman, "Financial situations, accomplishments, possessions, friendships and—coming in number one—their looks, especially when it comes to their weight."[38]

Part of the human struggle is comparison and jealousy. Even in the ancient history of Israel, King David recognized the struggle and penned these words: "Do not fret because of evildoers, be not envious toward wrongdoers. For they will wither quickly like the grass and fade like the green herb" (Psalm 37:1-2). And then David gave the salve for such fretting: "Rest in the Lord and wait patiently for Him; do not fret because of him who prospers in his way because of the man who carries out wicked schemes" (Psalm 37:7).

David's teaching began by addressing the problem of fretting over someone else's success or envying those who get away with injustice, but it didn't stop there. We all have a natural compass for fairness, but we also envy people for all kinds of good things too. Is there any better breeding ground for that than in social media? David's advice for envy still rings true:

> *"Trust in the LORD and do good; dwell in the land*
> *and cultivate faithfulness. Delight yourself in the*
> *LORD; and He will give you the desires of your*
> *heart. Commit your way to the LORD, trust also*
> *in Him, and He will do it. He will bring forth your*
> *righteousness as the light and your judgment as*
> *the noonday."* (Psalm 37:3-6).

Translation? Embrace contentment. Besides, here's the truth about our social media interaction: it's all a lie anyway! One snapshot from my day, one quote from my morning does not encapsulate all that is me. By design it's a misrepresentation! Here's a pretty picture of the flowers blooming outside my patio. It's what I've chosen for you to know about me, but I've also enhanced the color, sharpened the effects, brushed off a few cobwebs, and repositioned a plant or two. I'm dictating the context you have for me by presenting one picture and ignoring others. I didn't take a picture of the dead mouse just five feet from those flowers, for example. I didn't show you the woodpile in disarray or the plants wilting from lack of attention. I want you to think I live in flowerful Beauty Land. Have you ever lamented that your vacations aren't as wonderful as what you see on Instagram or Facebook? A recent travel survey found that over seventy percent of people exaggerate about their holidays, claiming to have more fun than they felt, boasting better weather, fancier hotels, and so on than what was experienced.

Social media, with all its filtering, virtue-signaling, and posturing, is crafted to misrepresent. Don't forget that when you compare your life to a snapshot of someone else. Turn around and ask yourself, how authentic are my posts? Have I embellished to the point of exaggeration or straight-out lying? Revolutionize your sharing by observing your motivation for posting and the outcomes you seek. A more gracious and authentic world begins with you and me!

Shun Overconsumption

Did you know that overconsumption of social media, clickbait, and bloggers inflates the ego and stirs a hunger for drama? Yes, we all love to hear ourselves talk. Are we any different from the first-century religious people whom Jesus condemned when He said, "Woe to you Pharisees! For you love the chief seats in the synagogues and the respectful greetings in the marketplaces" (Luke 11:43). Only now, we love scoring the most likes, a more significant following, or multiple comments and shares. The heart remains the same.

A lack of likes and comments triggers insecurity and feels like a personal rejection the entire world is witnessing. The whole platform teeters toward an emotionally disruptive experience. Even if we keep our emotions in check, I sense a dehumanizing impact from too much online exposure. I know many young women who have dropped social media entirely because they couldn't stand the drama, fighting, and posturing.

The Apostle Paul used a phrase that pricks my heart. He described those who are "always learning and never able to come to the knowledge of the truth" (2 Timothy 3:7).

Why the catch in my throat when I read that? Online, I feel I'm always absorbing and learning. I'm reading interesting blogs and thoughtful articles, skimming headlines along with catchy sayings and memes, spotting topics colliding with culture, and eavesdropping on the real scorcher articles of the day.

During this online media bombardment, I tussle with "always learning and never able to come to the knowledge of the truth." I feel informed, perhaps in touch with the world and my finger on the pulse of society, but I also feel disquieted and somehow disconnected. It's akin to the bloat and regret I feel after eating an entire bag of potato chips!

The toxic concoction of what we take in online snags our hearts and often our theology. It's toxic to our souls. Let's find a healthier and happier way to pursue knowledge so that we can cultivate the soil of gracious living.

Establish Boundaries

A starting point for gracious social media behavior is clearly defining what's out of bounds. Decide what's not ok with you and what types of interaction are acceptable. Reconfigure your online community by boundaries you set. Likely that will mean unfollowing some people and sites and perhaps even unfriending a few individuals.

For example, I think cursing and name-calling are out of bounds for a gracious person. The appeal to "Let no unwholesome word proceed from our mouth, but only such a word as is good for edification" (Ephesians 4:29) surely chaffs many online discussions. I don't participate in discussions that involve name-calling and cursing because I don't want to lend credibility there.

Proverbs 17:14 supports the quest for practical wisdom: "The beginning of strife is like letting out water, so abandon the quarrel before it breaks out." And Proverbs 26:20 offers proper online protocol: "For lack of wood, the fire goes out, and where there is no whisperer, contention quiets down." Creating and propagating contentions are out of bounds for any gracious peacebuilder. As Christ-followers, here's a simple, practical way to establish gracious boundaries for social media: Don't throw wood into the fire. Don't click, like, or share contentious material!

Paul Graham, a computer scientist and author, deposits this nugget of truth: "Things that lure you into wasting your time have to be really good at tricking you. An example that will be familiar to a lot of people is arguing online. When someone contradicts you, they're in a sense attacking you, sometimes pretty overtly. Your instinct, when attacked, is to defend yourself. But like a lot of instincts, this one wasn't designed for the world we now live in. Counterintuitive as it feels, it's better most of the time not to defend yourself. Otherwise these people are literally taking your life."[39]

In a nutshell, if your discussions degenerate into accusation and disrespect, take it offline. Suppress that human inclination to defend and attack.

Surprisingly, calls for restraint and kind, respectful discourse online are not from pastors and religious thought leaders but computer scientists and secular bloggers. That's a warning flare! In the church's pursuit of being cool, we forfeit our moral sense and authority in the world.

And speaking of morals, Scripture says that the deeds of the flesh are evident (Galatians 5:19). They are obvious, clearly seen, and understood. The acts of the flesh are visible and observable, striking, glaring, and blatant. These deeds, listed in Galatians are: "immorality, impurity, sensuality, idolatry, sorcery, enmities, strife, jealousy, outbursts of anger, disputes, dissensions, factions, envying, drunkenness, carousing and things like these."

Paul concluded this list by stating: "those who practice such things will not inherit the kingdom of God." These glaring behaviors may be something we stumble into on occasion, but they are not the social media practice or ongoing lifestyle of a believer.

I would guess that most click-bait is enticing either from a contentious angle or a sensual perspective. Do I need to say that pornography is out of bounds not only for a spiritual person, but for a compassionate, gracious, non-religious person as well? With one click, we aid and abet an industry that destroys lives, especially the young girls and boys filmed in porn. One click! My friend, it's not worth the destruction of your sexuality or the exploitation of another human being. Do whatever is necessary to protect yourself from this insidious addiction.

Recognize Saturation Points

One vital aspect of gracious social media behavior is an awareness of saturation points. Hold the Galatians 5:19 list up next to your favorite websites, blogs, news outlets, TV shows, and social media. Let it be the plumb line for your online activities. Are you wasting precious hours of your life drenched with impurity, disputes, or envy?

Your saturation point may even arrive through the constant flow of "self-improvement" information. Too many parenting and marriage support sites, though intended as helpful and non-judgmental, evolve into wearying content.

You are responsible, according to Scripture, to "watch over your heart with all diligence for from it flow the springs of life." That passage in Proverbs continues, talking about not only our hearts but also our mouths, eyes, and feet—all body parts we manage through our intentions.

"Put away from you a deceitful mouth and put devious speech far from you. Let your eyes look directly ahead and let your gaze be fixed straight in front of you. Watch the path of your feet and all your ways will be established. Do not turn to the right nor to the left; turn your foot from evil" (Proverbs 4:24-27). This wisdom instructs us to put away any partnership or participation with deceit, envy, and evil. It guides us toward not only gracious living in social media, but also a more thoughtful, mindful stance in every aspect of life.

One day, when our children were in high school, Andy and I detected a change in our phones. Because our devices connected to the same Apple ID and cloud, somehow, our phones tangled online. All of our kids' texts, emails, and phone calls sizzled onto Andy's and my devices! Similarly, our texts broadcast to our kid's phones.

For several days, sheer entertainment erupted from this mix-up. Our kids were wide-eyed, seeing how some of my friends communicated about chores such as carpool and cooking. Although the kids tried to warn their friends about the new transparency, some spicy high school verbiage flamed through. As much fun as we had eavesdropping on each other, an important lesson transpired: we all gained accountability. We never knew which text or email might land on someone else's device, so discretion became our editor!

Think about it: What if every comment, like, or click you made were visible to a loved one? Wouldn't it engage greater wisdom, discretion, and sensitivity to your online behavior? A gentle reminder for gracious behavior is that "there is no creature hidden from His sight, but all things are open and laid bare to the eyes of Him with whom we have to do" (Hebrews 4:13). Gracious communication strives to react online with caution and wisdom. Seeking to bless, uplift, and encourage with every like, emoji, share, and post is the secret to gracious online behavior.

Seek the Real

In theory, I would never trade appearing as a snippet of someone's Facebook feed for a real relationship, although in today's culture, much of my online time devolves into precisely that. When hours are absorbed online, I need an offset to balance or neutralize that time and effect. I need human interaction. I need to look into another person's face, see their eyes and smile, feel their touch, and experience real-time communication without filters, emojis, or camera angles. If online time is dehumanizing, then I need an immersion in a respectful and gracious connection. I need to move my body, play with my dog, hug my kids, and talk with a friend. We all need to find our counterbalances.

Connected to this need is the increase in interpersonal social anxiety seen among today's college students. On campus, I've noticed after a ninety-minute gathering, many students begin to feel overwhelmed socially and need time alone—on their device. They are exhausted by personal interaction and seek solace in online social media interaction.

This behavior is evidence that our attention spans are not the only skills affected by social media. Our capacity for unfiltered eye-to-eye interaction is also impacted. Frequently now, I observe students sitting on the edges of the auditorium rather than in center seats because they feel safer near the exit. To clarify, this is their behavior not at some dreaded symposium, but at one of their favorite, most enjoyable events of the week! This is another warning flare. If you don't use a skill, you lose it, and that rings true for our social abilities offline. We must seek the real deal—face-to-face human interaction; otherwise, we devolve.

I drove by my childhood playground the last time I visited Houston. A safer and far cooler plastic structure replaced the fort. I guess they finally figured out that metal slides didn't work in Houston's hot climate. I predict that generations to come will view these early days of the Internet and social media with the same head-scratching. They'll wonder, *what were they thinking? They made things butt-scorching hot and unsafe.*

Don't be a part of the problem online. Instead, graciously live the solution. Defend against a divisive spirit by proactively seeking unity. Don't generate sensational or disingenuous material. Graciously encourage and affirm others and don't lend the credibility of your life to unworthy sites.

Let this be your prayer each day as you navigate online:

"Give us discernment to know when to pray,
When to speak out,
When to act,
And when to simply
Shut off our screens

And our devices,
And to sit quietly
In your presence,
Casting the burdens of this world
Upon the strong shoulders
Of the one who alone
Is able to bear them up."[40]

Meaningful Dialogue

1. What part of social media feels like a drag on your time and positivity?

2. Have you discovered ways to bless and encourage others through social media? What does it look like?

3. How do you set yourself up for success in online activities so that you have no regrets around anything said or time spent?

4. How much are comparison and envy a struggle in your social media experience?

5. Do you find yourself feeling angry and agitated after being online? Or sad and feeling less than everyone else? How do you process this and safeguard against it?

Declarations for Gracious Living

I have made a covenant with my eyes. (Job 31:1)

The words of my mouth and the meditations of my heart are pure before God. (Psalms 19:14)

God is teaching me to number my days so that I can present to Him a heart of wisdom. (Psalms 90:12)

14

Open Hands

"The wicked borrows and does not pay back,
but the righteous is gracious and gives."
PSALM 37:21

I'm not going to mince words here. I don't understand a Christian who isn't joyfully generous and actively caring for those in need. Caring for the downtrodden and oppressed is inherent to the Christian message. It's the why behind almost every what. It's why Christians initially founded nearly every hospital in America. It's why every Ivy League school (except Cornell) was established by Christians to train ministers and further the gospel. It's why in every country that Christians influence, we see a rise in the rights of women, a greater focus on the needs of the poor, and the expansion of educational opportunities for the needy.

God so loved the world that He what? *He gave.* And because He gave, we must give. God poured out His goodness on us so we can be blessings and light to the entire world! Think about that. God graced us for gracious generosity!

Now Tweet This

In a world bombarded by social media sludge, the gracious good sense of the Book of Proverbs is the Twitter feed we desperately need these days. Its tidbits of wisdom guide our behavior and anchor our money habits. Read these nuggets of God's wisdom concerning generosity:

"Honor the Lord from your wealth and from the first of all your produce; so your barns will be filled with plenty and your vats will overflow with new wine" (Proverbs 3:9-10). That's 103 characters less than the 280 Twitter character limit, but those words speak volumes! Just try outgiving God!

Here's another tweet at just 213 characters: "Do not withhold good from those to whom it is due, when it is in your power to do it. Do not say to your neighbor, 'Go and come back, and tomorrow I will give it,' when you have it with you" (Proverbs 3:27, 28). Scripture nailed it here. So, why do we treat people this way? Withholding and controlling are powerless weapons. Generosity, on the other hand, moves mountains.

With just a scant ninety-seven characters, Proverbs 11:25 overflows with wisdom about generosity: "The generous man will be prosperous, and he who waters will himself be watered." Proverbs 19:17 backs up that truth: "One who is gracious to a poor man lends to the Lord, and He will repay him for his good deed." The poor man doesn't repay, but God does!

Of course, any serious discussion about poverty must include dialogue about injustice. Proverbs 13:23 warns, "Abundant food is in the fallow ground of the poor, but it is swept away by injustice." Bryan Stevenson's famous March

2012 TED talk, "We need to talk about an injustice,"[41] echoes this ancient truth.

Proverbs 31:8-9 also beeches us: "Open your mouth for the mute, for the rights of all the unfortunate. Open your mouth, judge righteously, and defend the rights of the afflicted and needy." Our influence, our voices, and our financial support are powerful advocates for those in need.

I love the way Proverbs 31:20 paints a graceful portrait of a beautiful woman in just ninety-five strokes: "She extends her hand to the poor, and she stretches out her hands to the needy." Outstretched hands—can't you see this stunning woman who works diligently in and outside the home —and reaches out to help the needy? Generosity is beautiful, my friend.

Does your practice of gracious generosity and justice for the poor pale in comparison to these Scriptures? Or do these truths confirm your approach to life?

The Gold Standard of Generosity

I can't talk about gracious living without holding up the gold standard of generosity toward the poor and justice for the oppressed. Jesus honored, nurtured, and poured into those in need. The generosity of Jesus was holistic. He wouldn't let someone slide into hell with a full belly; he fed the masses while inspiring them to live under God's reign. Genuine graciousness cares for the whole person. As the emissaries of Christ, we can't merely care for the spiritual needs in our world; we must also care about the physical obstacles people face.

We are called to mirror to the world what we see God doing. We represent Jesus to everyone under our influence. God has lavished on us all that we need for life and godliness. Jesus became poor so that we could be rich. He suffered whip marks on His back so that we could be free from sickness and disease. He became sin on the cross so that we could be the righteousness of God. His example is our heritage and identity. We must be generous, not just to please God, but because generosity is our heritage. It's who we are in Christ! Only if we are following a rigid rule set rather than nurturing a genuine relationship with Christ could generosity be seen as one more thing on a to-do list rather than the natural expression of joy. Practicing gracious generosity should be exhilarating, my friend!

Play No Trumpets

Although our gracious generosity should abound, discretion lies at the heart of it. No wonder Scripture warns us so sternly about human nature that seeks recognition, thanks, and personal benefit. Jesus taught just the opposite: "Beware of practicing your righteousness before men to be noticed by them; otherwise, you have no reward with your Father who is in heaven. So, when you give to the poor, do not sound a trumpet before you, as the hypocrites do in the synagogues and in the streets, so that they may be honored by men. Truly I say to you, they have their reward in full" (Matthew 6:1-2).

Although the practice sounds laughable these days, trumpets announced gifts in the first century. But are we any different, posting selfie after selfie that trumpets our good deeds? Take not a single picture on your next mission trip and see if your flesh cries out.

Recently our pastor asked for a special gift to pay for a conference our church hosted. He made it clear, "I won't send you a keychain if you give. I won't send a coffee mug, and I won't put your name in the program! I want you to give generously and secretly like Scripture says and receive a blessing from

God." In other words, no trumpets. I think that's the right thing to do, don't you?

Wise Generosity

We should avoid bragging about our giving. However, we must not play the fool either. When I moved to California from Texas in 1989, I needed a car that would survive the trip. My students affectionately named my ratty old Honda the "turd mobile" due to its brown paint and black tinted windows (and perhaps because it was a crappy old car).

That Honda would have left me in the driest part of New Mexico, so I gladly exchanged it for a red Toyota Corolla FX16. I loved that car! It was a hot hatchback with a twin-cam engine and sixteen valves that could go from zero to sixty in ten seconds. I drove that fun machine all the way to California and, for a year, commuted across the Golden Gate Bridge every day to seminary.

When kids' car seats joined my ride, I handed the Toyota off to my husband and I sadly downgraded to a station wagon. He drove the FX16 past 160,000 miles on the odometer. It was still a great car, but eventually, he needed a pickup truck. At the time, we knew of a young man recently released from jail who was trying to make a fresh start. Among other things, he needed a car, so we sold him our FX16 for one dollar. We felt great to deposit this gift into his life! *Shoot*, we thought, *if he works hard for a few years, the car will last him till he's settled.* Three days later, we discovered he had traded our FX16 as a down payment on a brand-new Mustang! We felt so stupid! My husband had driven the FX16 when he was a finance executive at a major corporation, but that kid working at a grocery store believed he needed a better ride.

That was one of the first lessons we learned about being smart with our generosity. It's ok to put parameters on gifts. It's okay to ask questions, to have boundaries, and to designate how donated money, time, and resources are used. Here are a few practical guidelines for wise generosity:

• **Cultivate clarity.** A friend of mine offered to help in her child's classroom art session once a week. The teacher exclaimed, "Hallelujah!" and put my friend on the art schedule every day. She calmly and warmly let the teacher know that she could come once a week and not more. Sometimes, when the needs are great, people can unintentionally take more than we've offered. Cultivate clarity about what you are willing to give.

• **Create a margin.** Build generosity into your schedule and budget. I came across a fascinating passage while reading (of all places) in Leviticus 19: "Now when you reap the harvest of your land, you shall not reap to the very corners of your field, nor shall you gather the gleanings of your harvest. Nor shall you gather the fallen fruit of your vineyard; you shall leave them for the needy and the stranger. I am the Lord, your God." Leaving margin in our time and resources buys us the freedom to be generous. The Levitical law creates a brilliant culture of generosity and flourishing for everyone, rich and poor alike!

• **Capture the vision.** Ask God to show you ways, big and small, that you can invest in others. Set goals. My mother-in-law is in her eighties, and she teaches the neighborhood kids piano lessons—for free! She gives twenty lessons a week and celebrates the joy of realizing her vision: kids from all backgrounds can have the opportunity to learn to play the piano. From the beautiful culture she has created, generosity has sprung up in many forms. One of the families that receives lessons decided to bring her a meal every week. Now my mother-in-law receives a healthy, homemade meal from her delightful Muslim neighbors. They are learning the piano, and she is learning a new style of cooking!

• **Chip away at the details.** It's a joy to gift our hard-earned money and resources for a cause we cherish. Equally, it's a disappointment when we share hard-earned time and money and later discover the person or organization isn't quite what we thought.

Faithfully steward your resources by asking direct questions of an individual or non-profit. How much do you need to reach your goals? How much are you currently receiving? Do you have accountability or oversight? Can I talk with others who have known you and supported you in the past? How will my money be used? How can I know for sure that these things are happening? How much of my money goes to overhead or administrative costs? Can I give toward a specific project that you oversee?

You may wonder, *How many ways could generosity go wrong?* Plenty! Years ago, my husband and I visited an orphanage in the Philippines. We toured the area in the directors' truck, met the children and teachers, and had a lovely visit. Afterward, thinking that they could invest more in their teachers and staff, we gave a large financial gift. We assumed that our perception of the need was the same for them (it was rather obvious really). To our shock, they instead purchased a nicer truck for the director! You see, we had clarity on what we could give, we created margin in our lives that allowed generosity, and we even envisioned giving to orphans around the world. But we didn't press in on the details of how this money would be used and ended up feeling foolish.

The Fruits of Generosity

There are many ways generosity can go right. I remember an eight hour bus ride through India, watching the beautiful green countryside rolling before my eyes. Frequently though, between random speed bumps and avoiding cows that rambled about freely, I observed groups of women and small children feverishly working on the side of the road. They were smashing rocks with a tiny hammer to make gravel. Elementary-age children would then take the gravel in buckets and carry it to a nearby worksite.

Our entire family was traveling with an organization I deeply respect, Good News India. We were headed to a Dream Center that housed, fed, and educated 100 girls rescued from abandonment, poverty, and possible sex-trafficking. Sitting with those precious girls that night, I learned that many of them had toiled their childhood away, breaking up rocks and carrying gravel. They said that before the Dream Center rescued them, their stomachs were often empty and their environments were harsh. Because of many folks like us—who merely gave the equivalent of a month's Starbucks' budget—these precious girls won scholarships at the Dream Center, which gave them 24/7 care, protection, food, clothes, and most importantly, an education.

Even though the Dream Center bustled with housing and feeding 100 girls, the rooms were neat and clean. Girls were happy and well-adjusted, and the entire atmosphere exuded order, contentment, and joy. One of the older girls explained how education was the only way to break out of her caste and poverty. Her life blossomed under the thoughtful provisions of Good News India.

Do I feel good spending my money for results? I do. I love coming alongside excellent people dedicated to intentionally improve the lives of the poor and oppressed. I know it pleases God when His children love and serve one another. For every ounce of advocacy, time, and resources I've donated to Good News India, I've received 100 times more blessings by fulfilling my purpose in life.

Nurture Gracious Generosity

When our four children were under the age of seven, Andy and I chose character traits to intentionally nurture in them. Generosity was one of the top four. We were committed to helping our children discover opportunities to share time, money, and resources with those who might need it. We delighted in surprising an elderly neighbor with warm cookies and encouraging notes. We sang and hugged our way through nursing homes. We sponsored farming projects in India, bought blankets for orphanages in Russia, and personally delivered computers in the Philippines and India. Our kids witnessed a day-in-day-out lifestyle of looking for needs around us and purposing to make a difference in the world. What an adventure!

Our kids are now college-aged, and I can testify to the fruit of our plan. They are gracious, generous young people who look for opportunities to help others. They are generous in small ways with their friends and classmates and volunteer at Camp Kesem to help children impacted by their parent's cancer. They love traveling to Haiti, Mexico, and Peru to share their time, talent, and treasure with phenomenal people living in difficult circumstances.

In the past few years, there have surely been struggles, disappointments, and even heartache. However, I derive great joy in knowing that my family has enabled a few people in the world to live another day and to live well. We've enjoyed vacations, parties, and plenty of self-focus to be sure, but I'm glad we realized the beauty in generosity. I'm thankful that our children have grown to be generous people who care for the rights of the oppressed. Even with the mishaps, I don't regret one dime given away or one ounce of energy spent caring for others.

Here's how the Apostle Paul summed up giving: "He who sows sparingly will also reap sparingly, and he who sows bountifully will also reap bountifully" (2 Corinthians 9:6). We all know this intuitively, yet we must be reminded. If we give sparingly, we reap sparingly. Maybe we think that no one has taken the time to help us, but we must ask ourselves *Have we invested in others?* Perhaps we feel slighted at work, but have we praised anyone besides ourselves?

Throughout the years, I have discovered three traits about sowing: We reap *what* we sow, we reap *how much* we sow, and we reap *later and greater* than we sow. If we plant apples, we will not get oranges. But often we plant shriveled seeds of greed and selfishness to somehow expect generosity in return! Luke penned, "Give, and it will be given to you. They will pour into your lap a good measure—pressed down, shaken together, and running over. For by your standard of measure it will be measured to you in return" (Luke 6:38).

Not only do we reap what we sow and how much we sow, but also later than we sow. We plant zucchini, and we harvest in three months. We plant an oak tree, and it takes years to see growth. It's easy to forget this when we are kind to someone once and expect results tomorrow. We may give generously for years before we see a harvest. The hidden promise of sowing and reaping is that we reap more than what we put in. One apple seed doesn't return one apple to us; it returns exponentially more. Those acts of kindness and thoughtfulness return more kindness and goodness to us when we practice patience. When we build wells or houses or pay for food and education, the world reaps the good for generations to come.

Paul wrote in 2 Corinthians 9:8, "And God is able to make all grace abound to you, so that always having all sufficiency in all things you may have an abundance for every good deed." *All grace for all sufficiency in all things.* The word "all" in the Greek is fascinating; it means all. Seriously though, this concept revolutionizes our generosity. Why? Because God says we possess everything we need to do good things. Right now. Just as we are. We have enough, and we are enough. We have good to give.

You may be thinking *Hold up, wait a minute, Margaret. Maybe you have an abundance, but I'm worried I can't even pay my bills!* Even in tough times, through wise stewardship and wise generosity, we will prosper in our ways, and we will have an abundance for every good deed. We cannot give what we don't possess, but we can be generous with what we have: time, talent, and treasure. Somehow, just as God's word proclaims, good returns to us—pressed down, shaken together, and running over!

If you are someone who struggles with generosity or are sometimes frustrated by your own tight grip on things, here are a few suggestions that might help you break out:

• **Try saying yes more often.** Especially in the little things, follow the Proverb, "If it is in your power to do good, do not withhold it." And open up your life to opportunity disguised as interruption.

• **Give Secretly!** Don't tell anyone about it, and don't post your generosity with Facebook selfies. Privately giving or serving has long acted as a spiritual discipline for ancient believers. It tames that human nature to brag or receive credit.

• **Mirror what you see God doing around you.** If God has blessed you, then do the same for others. He longs to pour out good into your lap! He provides, protects, and replenishes. Try to do the same for the people around you.

• **Change your language.** All people bear the image of God. Speak of them with honor. Speak of yourself as honored to share, even if stingy behaviors robbed your harvest in the past. Compassion and generosity rewire not only our self-concept but our life direction as well. Every day speak the truth about your life: "I have been given all that I need for life and godliness" (2 Peter 1:3). "I lack no good thing" (Psalms 34:10). "The generous will be prosperous" (Proverbs 11:25).

My joy is complete when I see Christians around the world work to alleviate the pain and suffering of poverty and oppression. I'm proud to take the name of Christ-follower by joyfully giving and actively caring as He did for those in need. Will you join me in modeling gracious generosity?

Meaningful Dialogue

1. Was generosity modeled to you growing up? Does anyone in your life stand out to you as a compelling example of a graciously generous person?

2. Brainstorm some examples of generosity in the life of Jesus. How can you emulate these?

3. How do you plan generosity into your budget of time, talent, or treasure?

4. Is generosity an integral part of your walk with God now? Does giving or advocacy present a struggle in some ways?

Declarations for Gracious Living

I am blessed coming in and blessed going out! (Deuteronomy 28:6)

I have all that I need for life and godliness. (2 Peter 1:3)

I am a good steward of my time, talent and treasure. I abound in gracious works! (2 Corinthians 8:7)

PART THREE

Walking Your Path

"There has never been the slightest doubt in my mind
that the God who started this great work in you
would keep at it and bring it to a flourishing finish
on the very day Christ Jesus appears."

PHILIPPIANS 1:6

15

Beautiful Boundaries

*"Like a city that is broken into and without walls
is a man who has no control over his spirit."*

PROVERBS 25:28

Now for an important disclaimer: Gracious living isn't a rigid yardstick for 24/7 alignments. Put me in a situation where I haven't eaten, I'm cold and need coffee, or I've said *yes* far too many times, and you'll see me flying on a broom. Gracious will not describe me. That's why boundaries are so vital. Without them, we God-gals will aim for Grace Goddess—until we're not, and stuff starts flying.

Remember my friend, Regina, whose spaghetti sauce exploded all over her kitchen? Before that fateful day, with overboard kindness, she squeaked out a *yes* to almost any request:

"Can we have our group meeting at your house, Regina?"

"Sure!"

"Can you make dinner for everyone?"

"Love to!"

"Can you lead the Bible study this week?"

"Oh, ok."

"Can you print the pages for everyone?"

"Deep sigh, yes."

When someone is willing to do all the heavy lifting, it's so easy to let them. (Sad, but true.)

After that explosive night, Regina realized she cared too much about what others thought about her and not enough about what she needed. As she started carrying less of the load for our group, the rest of us had the opportunity to lift more. That shift opened up clear ownership of our group vision, along with a deeper commitment to one another. It helped our group that Regina did less!

The Struggle with Boundaries

In a world filled with so many requests—and what feels like flat-out demands—how do God-girls decide what gets, as author Lysa Terkeurst puts it, "our best *yes*"? It's a puzzle for sure.

We women of faith often battle guilt if we don't help others; however, at times, we can also feel taken advantage of, wondering if we should "put our foot down" on perpetual requests or inconsiderate behavior. Many of us struggle with the entire concept of boundaries.

Is it okay to set limits?

What if those boundaries hurt people?

Isn't it selfish to set a limit with people I care about?

Shouldn't I always be willing to give to those who ask?

A lot of squirming goes on amidst the audacity of saying *no* while being loving, giving, and servant hearted.

In the past, I wrestled long and hard with boundary balance with family, friends, and ministry leaders. I entertained a lot of thoughts that had no boundaries:

I'm a Christian, so I should focus on other people, not myself.

I shouldn't need my own way.

I should be willing to give of myself whenever asked.

You can always give more, Margaret!

You have an unlimited capacity to love, serve, and give.

Those mindsets had me sliding down the wall far too many times, looking like Regina's exploded spaghetti sauce!

Scripture seems to add to the confusion about boundaries. Galatians 6:2 tells us, "carry each other's burdens and thus fulfill the law of Christ." But just a few sentences further, Galatians 6:5 states, "each one should carry their own load." Well, which is it: carry each other's burden or lug our own load?

The only way to solve this inconsistency is to trace those passages back to their Greek origins. The Greek word for burden means something that weighs us down beyond what we can carry. When Paul wrote, "carry each other's burden," he was saying, be concerned about one another! When you see someone struggling under a weight that's too heavy, help them out!

But the Greek word for load in Galatians 6:5 means cargo or everyday work. Paul said, "each one should carry their own load," meaning that each person is responsible for toting their own everyday-life stuff!

While it's true that, in Christ, we gals can do all things (Philippians 4:13), we must ask ourselves some straightforward questions:

What is truly loving?

Is it loving to take someone's daily load, so they never develop the muscle and capacity to do it themselves?

Is it loving to accommodate other's sin and dysfunction, so they never grow or change?

Is it loving to carry things we're not called to carry and then fail in our responsibilities? Is it loving to live small— to try not to take up space in conversations, demands, or wants— to hide our light behind others?

The answer to all these questions is a big fat *NO!*

Translation? Real friends don't perpetually dump their everyday stuff on others—out of convenience, inconsideration, dysfunction, or (dare I say) outright laziness. They also don't perpetually pick up the everyday load of others out of a distorted view of service and grace. But when life caves in with weighty rocks of trouble, trial, and burden, real friends roll up their sleeves and lift with gracious muscle. They're all-in to help carry the weight of another for a time!

Beautiful Walls of Self-Value

Grasping the importance and vitality of gracious boundaries does require self-value. It took me years flooded with resentment and guilt to finally embrace a golden nugget of revolutionary, foundational wisdom:

> *I am a human being worthy of love and respect.*
> *My wants, desires, dreams, and goals are equally*
> *important to those of others.*

Let me repeat that statement as it is revolutionary for many of us:

My wants, desires, dreams, and goals are equally important to anyone else's.

Where beautiful, gracious boundaries are concerned, a self-value framework is vital. If our *yes* is to be an exuberant "*hell-yes!*" and our no a firm and healthy *no*, then we need God-given, self-awareness reasoning behind our decisions. In their timeless book *Boundaries: When to Say Yes, and How to Say No to Take Control of Your Life*, Dr. Henry Cloud and Dr. John Townsend provide that reasoning:

> *"Being created in God's image also means having ownership, or stewardship. As Adam and Eve were given dominion over the earth to subdue and rule it, we are also given stewardship over our time, energy talent, values, feelings, behavior, money."*[42]

By God's design, stewardship is personal, my friend. The great work of gracious boundaries includes a personal affirmation that each of us should speak daily to ensure gracious boundary lines stay set:

> *I'm in charge of me! I can't change other people. Like a property line, boundaries define what's mine— what's inside my responsibility and what isn't. Inside my property, I'm in charge of what happens. Outside my property, I'm not in charge.*

The truth is, to be able to serve others graciously, we must maintain stewardship clarity about ourselves. You see, gracious living is about creating honor and beauty for ourselves and others.

A while ago, I dreamed that my house was whole and beautiful along the front and sides, but at the back corner, the walls were completely open and unfinished. For several nights, this dream returned in various forms.

Finally, I asked the Lord, *What's the meaning of this dream?* God showed me that I possessed thoughtful, intentional boundaries in many aspects of my life. I rarely found myself overextended in commitments outside the home. However, there was a side that was completely open and undeveloped. It was on the backside of my house that anyone could wander in and make a mess!

Often in that dream, kids were playing soccer inside. Parties of my friends would appear, and I wouldn't be ready. People would park their cars inside my house—and so on. In my dream, I would wrestle with the intrusion, but it was God who showed me that I needed boundaries. I needed to complete the construction of my home on all sides. I needed to steward my walls.

In Isaiah 49:16, God lovingly says, "Behold, I have inscribed you on the palms of My hands; Your walls are continually before Me." In Isaiah's time, walls defined a city. They kept the good in and the bad out. When God said, "Your walls are continually before Me," He was saying, *I care about your protection. I care about how your life is defined. I want My good to rest within your walls, and I want bad things blocked from entering or interfering.*

Here's how that dream impacted me on a practical basis: I love serving my family. Cooking for them, hosting parties, and making their lives seamless are big ways I demonstrate my love. But when doing their errands or chores means I don't have time, energy, or creativity for my life, it's a lose-lose situation. They lose the opportunity to manage their lives like adults, and I miss out on leading my life with focus.

Getting clear about my self-value—and the boundaries connected to it—helped me become a more gracious wife and mom. For example, I used to make dinner for everyone, and they would immediately exit after we finished eating. Leaving me to clean up solo, resentment started banging at my door. I soon learned to say to my loved ones, "Many hands make the work light; let's all finish these dishes before we run out." And the practice soon became organic for everyone. Gracious boundaries are the antidote for resentment.

Gracious boundaries can be life-giving for marriage too. When the kids were young, it was important to me that we ate dinner together as a family. Night after night, I found myself delaying the meal, not knowing when Andy would get home from work. The kids would be grumpy, tired, and hungry. I tried controlling Andy's behavior by complaining, threatening, withdrawing, and so on. The tell-tale guest of resentment pretty much parked itself in our home!

Finally, I realized I could not control Andy; I could only control myself. I warmly told him that I would love for all of us to share dinnertime, and it would be served between 6:30 and 7:00 each night. Did he push back on my clarity? Sure! Now and then, he would call and say, "I'm on my way! Wait for me!" Sometimes, I'd fall for it. Then a call or some distraction would delay him further. I'd quickly remember why I had the dinner boundary in place. It was a love thing! Cloud and Townsend so get this reality!

> "Remember that a boundary always deals with yourself, not the other person. Do not confuse boundaries with a new way to control a spouse. It is the opposite. It is giving up control and beginning to love. You are giving up trying to control your spouse and allowing him to take responsibility for his own behavior."[43]

With that wisdom in mind, grab this truth and hold it close: Establishing boundaries does not reflect a lack of love or commitment. It's just the opposite! Since God calls each of us to steward our lives, we must do it well. I love the advice of Cloud and Townsend on this:

> *"Other people have wants and needs of their own, and we must negotiate a fair and loving relationship and respect each other's limits. The key here is that the other person is not responsible for our limits; we are. Only we know what we can and want to give, and only we can be responsible for drawing that line. If we do not draw it, we can quickly become resentful."*[44]

And boy, do I know it! Realizing I'm in charge of me and accountable for my attitudes and actions has brought freedom into my life, along with clarity.

These days, resentment rarely rears its ugly head in my life. I've learned to embrace the grace that boundaries release for me and others. Emerging from that learning curve are five solid principles. They can help all God-gals shake off guilt chains and celebrate the opportunities that boundaries provide.

• **The difference between selfishness and stewardship.** Clarity on this is vital! Selfishness is allegiance to one's goals, priorities, and wishes to the exclusion of caring for others. In an unrelenting, unswerving dedication to personal wishes above all else, selfishness ignores the burdens of others.

As a contrast, listen to what Cloud and Townsend say about stewardship:

> *"A helpful way to understand setting limits is that our lives are a gift from God. Just as a store manager takes good care of a shop for the owner, we are to do the same with our souls. If a lack of boundaries causes us to mismanage the store, the owner has a right to be upset with us. We are to*

*develop our lives, abilities, feelings, thoughts, and
behaviors. Our spiritual and emotional growth is
God's 'interest' on His investment in us. When we
say no to people and activities that are hurtful to
us, we are protecting God's investment."*[45]

I love that God calls me to steward what He has placed inside of me. I need to ensure that my life reflects the goodness God has given me to manage. We God-gals must understand the difference between effective giving and toxic enabling if we are to embody gracious living:

*"Favors and sacrifices are part of the Christian
life. Enabling is not. Learn to tell the difference by
seeing if your giving is helping the other to become
better or worse. The Bible requires responsible
action out of the one who is given to. If you do not
see it after a season, set limits (Luke 13:9)."*[46]

Thoughtfully responding *no* to a request enables the stewardship of God-given priorities. On saying *no*, Lysa TerKeurst, author of *The Best Yes,* says, "This doesn't make me a bad person. It makes me the wrong person for that assignment."[47] That is pure wisdom for the road of life, my friends!

• **Get to the heart of relational fears.** Creating honor and grace in a relationship cannot originate in fear, obligation, or manipulation. Absorbing this truth is a gamechanger! Many of us say *yes* out of fear, not love. Fear of abandonment, anger, loneliness, and payback can sometimes motivate us more than love. Boundaries can change that misguided thinking. Cloud and Townsend stress that clear boundaries not only guard against the resentful *yes* but also nurture the souls of those involved.

*"Often, we will privately endure the pain of
someone's irresponsibility instead of telling them
how their behavior affects us and other loved ones,
Information that would be helpful to their soul."*[40]

You see, boundaries are a love gift for us and others. They
feed souls starved for honesty and clarity! That perspective is
both calming and life-giving.

If fear keeps us quiet on confronting others, it can also
propel us to waver in our decisions. At best such dithering
confuses others. Far worse, it can fuel their selfish, manipula-
tive behavior, which is detrimental for them and us! The Bible
clearly instructs about clarity and firmness: "but your *yes* is to
be *yes*, and your *no, no* so that you may not fall under judgment" (James 5:12b). Wavering does not reflect the grounding
of solid, biblical principles, so learning to maintain a steward-
ed *no* is essential for gracious living.

Last but not least, fear can also entangle us in webs of unrealistic expectations. I love Lysa Terkeurst's take on this:

*"You won't ever be able to keep up with unreal-
istic. Unrealistic demands lead to undercurrents
of failure. So, don't allow the unrealistic demands
of others to march freely into your life. Resolve
instead to make decisions based on what is re-
alistic—not on trying to earn the approval of or
impress another."*[49]

• **Define your values.** Confession time: I used to struggle with
a feeling of over-responsibility for those who were hurting.
Yet, I possessed little awareness of my needs. Years ago, when
the subject of hopes and dreams came up in my small group,
I couldn't think of a single one! *What were my hopes and
dreams, my desires?* I realized my life had been others-orient-
ed, so much so that I had no idea what I wanted. In essence, I

had failed to define my values and dreams, which, in turn, created a boundary vacuum. Without acknowledged goals, I had nothing to protect! I would knee-jerk react to the requests of others rather than respond from an awareness of my dreams and the boundaries that supported and protected them.

Life and the counsel of wise mentors taught me that knowing who God designed me to be and where I'm headed based on my values is the best GPS ever created! And like a GPS, Cloud and Townsend encourage a pre-emptive mindset where goals and boundaries are concerned:

> *"Become proactive. Instead of allowing someone else to be in control, figure out what you want to do, set your course, and stick to it. Decide what your limits are, what you will allow yourself to be a party to, what you will no longer tolerate, and what consequences you will set. Define yourself proactively, and you will be ready to maintain your boundaries when the time comes."*[50]

Such a proactive mindset will likely incur applause as well as some unpleasant pushback that requires a gracious and controlled response. The latter is a muscle I've had to build over the years. Cloud and Townsend have their fingers on the pulse of disrespected boundaries and offer this wisdom for life in the trenches.

> *"Boundaries are a 'litmus test' for the quality of our relationships. Those people in our lives who can respect our boundaries will love our wills, our opinions, our separateness. Those who can't respect our boundaries are telling us that they don't love our no. They only love our yes, our compliance."*[51]

"Respond rather than react. "The difference
between responding and reacting is choice. When
you are reacting, they are in control. When you
respond, you are."[32]

• **Know your "mine."** In 2001, our family of six lived in a 1550 square feet home. The kids were ages six, five, three, and one. The three girls shared a small bedroom. They each had one drawer in the dresser for their clothes plus a tiny closet for shoes and coats. Under the religious teaching that "mine" reflects a selfish, inherent sin nature, I rankled every time my children yelled, "That's mine!" I would think, *When you don't share, you are selfish and self-centered. My job is to coach you away from your sinful, prideful, possessive, little heart!*

I didn't realize back then that children need to develop a "no" and a "mine" to establish boundaries and a sense of self. Sure, we all have to learn to share, but we also need to learn that our words have power. Our boundaries define us.

• **Celebrate freedom love.** A missionary friend of ours was jailed in another country and later proven innocent. Two months of being packed into a cell with twenty-eight men taught some great lessons. He's one of the most generous and kind men I've ever known, so I was surprised to hear that he got into a fistfight with someone trying to steal his blanket! Bloodied and bruised, he kept his blanket for the night. The next morning, he gave the blanket to his astonished opponent, saying, "I will give my blanket to you, but you cannot take it from me."

For me, this story beautifully defines gracious boundaries: giving what I have chosen to provide—free of any fear, obligation, or manipulation. However, pressuring me to do what discomforts me or give what I want to keep will not meet success.

Discernment about giving is really quite simple, and TerKeurst beautifully phrases it: "We must not confuse the command to love with the disease to please."[53]

When I'm clear about what I want to give—whether it's my time, energy, money, friendship, whatever—I can intentionally love and serve people with my whole heart. That's the freedom of gracious boundaries.

I continually hear about needs around the world. There are also perpetual needs within my family, community, and country. Amid all this need, I have the honor and responsibility to give, influence, and serve others as I choose. The Apostle Paul said it well, "And this is my prayer: that your love may abound more and more in knowledge and depth of insight, so that you may be able to discern what is best and may be pure and blameless for the day of Christ" (Philippians 1:9-10).

Oh, how I love Paul's prayer! It's the perfect affirmation for God's gals. May our love for others abound more and more—and may we be able to discern what is best.

Often, I pray for my love not to wane but to shine on through the darkness. I've wondered how Jesus could sleep at night when He had only healed a percentage of the population and transformed a limited number of people. Yet, he never fretted or panicked. Instead, He walked with purpose and intentionality through the throngs of people. In love and perseverance, He ended His time on earth with three simple words, "It is finished." Jesus discerned what was best. He completed what God sent Him here to do. He lived his "mine" and celebrated that freedom love.

My friend, I pray that you also will live according to God's purpose for your life. May you graciously fulfill the good works God prepared for you, knowing your "mine" and celebrating the freedom of love's boundaries. Never forget, "For we are His workmanship, created in Christ Jesus for good works, which God prepared beforehand so that we would walk in them" (Ephesians 2:10).

Meaningful Dialogue

1. Where in your life do you find it challenging to hold boundaries?

2. Do you ever struggle with your needs seeming to be less important than the needs of others?

3. What are gracious ways you have set up boundaries?

4. What relationship in your life needs more honor and grace extended rather than limits? Do you feel called to give and serve in any particular area?

5. What is the hardest part of living with boundaries? What's the best part?

Declarations for Gracious Living

I do good to all people for whatever I sow I also reap. (Galatians 6:7,10)

I am God's workmanship, created in Christ Jesus for good works. (Ephesians 2:10)

I watch over my heart and steward my life with all diligence. (Proverbs 4:23)

16

Overcoming Obstacles

*"May the Lord of peace Himself continually
grant you peace in every circumstance."*
2 Thessalonians 3:16

I wish you and I could nestle into my comfy couch and unfurl all the hurts, insecurities, and fears that trigger our ungracious responses. Life can wear down God-gals, even the most resilient. We build walls to block out pain—and end up erecting obstacles to gracious behavior. But with tenderness and compassion, God will uproot any hurt, unforgiveness, or bitter spirit if we ask Him. First, though, we must examine the hindrances to the goal of living graciously. Then, we can partner with God as we release any unforgiveness or hurts that we carry.

My friend Caroline earnestly seeks a gracious spirit, and in many situations, she is a jewel—funny, generous, and thoughtful. Some days though, Caroline's past floods her present.

Childhood trauma echoes in her mind like flying shrapnel, disrupting her sleep, work, and relationships. The shaming her parents dished out, along with their searing judgments and physical abuse, shackled my friend long after she moved away from her childhood home.

Caroline's insecurity rears its head in various ways. She is meticulous with her outward appearance, but shame floods her if others dress better than she does. Whenever confronted with anguish she has inflicted or a mistake she has made, Caroline completely shuts down, offering no apology or empathy. She then plummets into self-loathing. As a leading trauma specialist put it, "Being traumatized is not just an issue of being stuck in the past; it is just as much a problem of not being fully alive in the present."[54]

My sweet friend is doing the hard work of healing her soul so that she can become fully alive in the present and live the abundant life Christ offers. It's a slow, intentional journey. Through loving support and encouragement, Caroline is slowly marching toward health, wholeness, forgiveness, and gracious living.

Beliefs That Hinder Gracious Living

Like Caroline, all of us identify with the pain of rejection, failure, fear, and shame. We possess an ideal of who we long to become, but alas, we haven't yet arrived. Most of us set our sights on graciousness, but insecurities derail us. We deny the impact of past anguish, or we "take the edge off" with alcohol, excessive exercise, overeating, working insane hours, or simply binge-watching Netflix®. Like that old Jackson Browne song laments, though, "No matter how fast I run, I can never seem to get away from me."[55]

So, let's stop running and face the beliefs that keep us stuck. When we examine our unconscious beliefs, it's like throwing open the curtains to let the sunshine pour into a dark room. Shame evaporates in the light. The demons of fear, rejection, and unforgiveness must flee. When our past heals, our present is redeemed—and our future starts looking hopeful.

God lovingly comes alongside us in this journey, encouraging us in "casting all your anxiety on Him, because He cares for you" (1 Peter 5:7). But first, we need clarity about what we are casting on Him. See if your heart resonates with any of the following toxic beliefs that impede gracious living. Then I'll show you how to weed them out of your life.

• **The bad behavior belief:** *Failure in myself and others must be punished—or it will increase!* This toxic creed asserts that we should not be gracious to people who don't work for it. Letting people off the hook can be an intense struggle. Many of us harshly pinpoint and punish any mistake. But we misconstrue grace when we are overly concerned about others getting away with bad behavior. Does this punishment mindset block gracious words and actions? You bet it does!

• **The victim belief:** *Life has beaten me up, so I have nothing to give. The world owes me—or at least should give me a break. I'm so depleted and emotionally bankrupt no one should expect me to give anything. Others might call me narcissistic, but I'm in such pain, I need care more than anyone.* Could this victim mindset deter graciousness? Absolutely! As Jesus said, it is out of the abundance of the heart that we speak. If the victim mindset saps our thinking, we won't have an abundance of love and grace from which to live.

• **The can't let it go belief:** *When someone hurts me, I'm not going to forget it. I carry the hurt and pain from events and* *relationships. Other people "get over it," but I can't let go.* Does unforgiveness stall gracious living? No doubt about it!

• **The defensive belief:** *If I'm gracious and kind, others will take advantage of me.* Fear erects a tough exterior to hide vulnerability. Self-protection efforts keep defenses up all the time out of fear of getting hurt. Can fear block graciousness? Yes, fear hides the best in us.

We know from Jesus' words in John 15 that God will prune anything in us that isn't bearing good fruit. And it's His kindness that does the pruning. When we partner with fear, shame, unforgiveness, bitterness, and self-pity, we remain connected to the anguish we are trying to flee. But God, in His great love and mercy, is committed to helping us cut the ties that bind us to our sin and others' sins against us.

My friend, aren't you thankful God provides a path to abundant living and freedom from false belief? When we partner with His presence, God shows us how to be victoriously free in His love.

Caroline and I, along with many other women, have learned how to partner with God in clearing our hurts. We are walking in more freedom than we ever imagined possible. The way I partner with Him is through five practices: forgiving, filling, declaring, sharing, and communion. Walk with me through each of these. It's the path to removing the obstacles to gracious living.

The Forgiveness Process

Forgiveness isn't for sissies. Jesus' words to a frustrated Peter reveal this truth: "Then Peter came and said to Him, 'Lord, how often shall my brother sin against me and I forgive him? Up to seven times?' Jesus said to him, 'I do not say to you, up to seven times, but up to seventy times seven'" (Matthew 18:21-22).

Can you imagine the thud of this statement? Jewish law dictated a three-strikes scenario. Peter, stretching to the limits of his human thinking, doubled it and added one for good measure. "Should I forgive someone seven times?" The old boy got the equivalent of a slap in the face when Jesus gave him a lesson in God's math. Our natural capacity for forgiveness is seemingly not worth squat, and Jesus told a story to illustrate why.

> *"For this reason, the kingdom of heaven may be compared to a king who wished to settle accounts with his slaves. When he had begun to settle them, one who owed him ten thousand talents was brought to him. But since he did not have the means to repay, his lord commanded him to be sold, along with his wife and children and all that he had, and repayment to be made. So, the slave fell to the ground and prostrated himself before him, saying, 'Have patience with me and I will repay you everything.' And the lord of that slave felt compassion and released him and forgave him the debt. But that slave went out and found one of his fellow slaves who owed him a hundred denarii; and he seized him and began to choke him, saying, 'Pay back what you owe.' So, his fellow slave fell to the ground and began to plead with him, saying, 'Have patience with me and I will repay you.' But he was unwilling and went and threw him in prison until he should pay back what was owed. So, when his fellow slaves saw what had happened, they were deeply grieved and came and reported to their lord all that had happened. Then summoning him, his lord said to him, 'You wicked slave, I*

forgave you all that debt because you pleaded with me. Should you not also have had mercy on your fellow slave, in the same way that I had mercy on you?" And his lord, moved with anger, handed him over to the torturers until he should repay all that was owed him. My heavenly Father will also do the same to you, if each of you does not forgive his brother from your heart." (Matthew 18:23-35)

Rather than a stern rebuke, I sense the love from Jesus as He told Peter this story. He knew the tortuous imprisonment that comes with unforgiveness. Jesus connected our forgiving others to God's forgiveness of us. He used exaggeration to communicate seriousness. The first slave owed something like the national debt—insurmountable! Instead of overflowing with joy and generosity, he seemed angered and stringently committed to leveling scores. When he bullied his fellow slave for the equivalent of a day's wage, it was as if he didn't own that he was forgiven and set free.

Many of us also struggle with forgiveness. Cognitively, we understand that Jesus paid our debt; we are forgiven and accepted in Christ, yet we don't live from that posture. We may feel we have to fight for our rights to ensure others do not take us for granted or abuse us. In this parable, Jesus said unforgiveness results in torture. Anyone who has ever lived under the weight of unforgiveness can attest that the torture part is a reality. Our hearts cannot carry such burdens! Unforgiveness keeps us tied to offenses and fearful, thus attracting more offense.

Paul gently urged us:

"Be kind to one another, tender-hearted, forgiving each other, just as God in Christ also has forgiven you." (Ephesians 4:32).

> *"Bearing with one another, and forgiving each*
> *other, whoever has a complaint against anyone;*
> *just as the Lord forgave you, so also should you."*
> (Colossians 3:13)

From these Scriptures, as well as the Matthew 18 parable, we see that forgiveness links with the cross of Christ. Because He loved us and willingly gave His life on the cross to purchase our forgiveness, we are empowered to love and forgive as well. We didn't earn or deserve the forgiveness Christ purchased at the cross. Some of us didn't even desire it, but forgiveness and the cancelation of debts still remain available.

Forgiving others, saying they don't owe us anything, is based on one first-person fact: *Christ forgave us and commanded us to forgive others.* That's it. Conditional forgiveness enslaves. If someone says, *I'll forgive her when she apologizes and makes it right again,* that behavior entangles with another's behavior. If one minimizes a wound and thinks, *Well, he was doing the best he could with his upbringing,* that's excusing, not forgiving.

Robert McGee summarizes the forgiveness concept well in his book *Search for Significance*:

> *"Sometimes we think that forgiveness is somewhat*
> *like a large eraser that wipes our offenses off the*
> *books. However, God never has forgiven like this.*
> *For each offense, He demanded full payment. This*
> *is the reason for the cross. Christ has paid for our*
> *sins in full."*[56]

To thoroughly work through the forgiveness process, I need a pen and paper, so grab those, along with a box of Kleenex, and let's hang on to each other as we forgive the hurts and injustices against us. This process takes some time, so carve out sacred moments when you will not be interrupted. (I must pause here and thank my professor at Fuller Seminary, Dr. Charles Kraft for teaching me so much about forgiveness and how it heals the heart. His passion for healing was fresh air for my stagnant soul, and his principles are at the core of the forgiveness process that follows.)

• I begin by thanking God for forgiving my sins and the ways I've betrayed Him and those I love. I anchor in His love and kindness for me. Then, I ask God to show me any hurts, offense, and unforgiveness I am hoarding toward anyone. I write down what He brings to mind, listing the person, the offense, and all the effects this hurt has had in my life. I list the emotions that came with that hurt—perhaps betrayal, anger, fear, loss of joy or security, and so on.

• For each offense and all that it involved, I acknowledge that Jesus is just, and He will deal with that person in His perfect will. I acknowledge that Jesus died on the cross to pay for that offense with His precious blood. I don't excuse or minimize what has been done to me. Theophostic counselor Ed Smith offers this guidance: "Before true forgiveness can be given, a wounded person must understand clearly what the debt is that he needs to forgive and why he needs to release it. True forgiveness is a consequence of taking an account of the debt that a person is owed."[57]

Then, I take the offense, hurt, and every connected emotion, and lay them at the feet of Jesus. Each time I say something like, *I have every right to be hurt (angry, bitter, jealous, afraid), but I know if I hold on, it will ruin me. It's too heavy for me to carry, Lord.* I ask Jesus to carry that hurt or offense for me.

• I acknowledge that the hurt has taken up space in my heart and mind that needs to be filled with something else. If I've held bitterness, for example, I will ask Jesus to replace it with a sweet and tender spirit. If I've held on to fear and foreboding, I'll ask Jesus to pour joy in every place that once carried fear.

• Because demonic spirits often inflame unforgiveness, I conclude my forgiveness practice with a prayer of renunciation and protection. I'll pray, *I no longer partner with unforgiveness (bitterness, fear, anger, hurt). I command these spirits to leave in Jesus' name. I forbid them to return or torment me about this hurt again.* The Apostle Paul alluded to this in 2 Corinthians 2:10-11: "But one whom you forgive anything, I forgive also; for indeed what I have forgiven, if I have forgiven anything, I did it for your sakes in the presence of Christ, so that no advantage would be taken of us by Satan, for we are not ignorant of his schemes."

Satan often ensnares through unforgiveness. Therefore, I urge, along with Paul, that we forgive any offense so that Satan won't be empowered to take advantage of us.

Holy Spirit Resurfacing

My practice of filling, or what I call Holy Spirit Resurfacing, comprises a few moments each night as I drift off to sleep. We all know that we live from our experiences. If I experience abandonment, for example, I will live from a posture of abandonment, fearing relationship losses in spite of signs of stability. If I experience tremendous strife, I will live from that experience and think every minor disagreement is a war.

When I go to bed, I ask for a deeper experience in the Holy Spirit than what I had during the day. I'll breathe words like this: *"I want to live from a deeper experience, Lord! I want to live from a posture of great love and compassion! I want to live from graciousness and kindness through You, Jesus."* Then, from the God of all mercy and kindness, the God who longs to pour out good on me, I ask: *"Holy Spirit, please fill any place in me that is low or depleted. Give me a greater experience in You than what I have experienced in the world today."*

These words comprise my last prayer every night before I go to sleep, and they work miracles. Why would we not ask for this? He is the God who fills in every valley and makes low every mountain. The crooked shall become straight, and the rough ways smooth (Luke 3:5). If God can do this to landscape, He can smooth out some bumpy ground in me!

Isaiah 54:1 evokes this Holy Spirit resurfacing: "Shout for joy, O barren one, you who have borne no child; break forth into joyful shouting and cry aloud, you who have not travailed; for the sons of the desolate one will be more numerous than the sons of the married woman," says the Lord. And then there's verse four: "Fear not, for you will not be put to shame; and do not feel humiliated, for you will not be disgraced; but you will forget the shame of your youth, and the reproach of your widowhood you will remember no more."

Supernatural restoration overwhelms the natural, physical limitations of our lives. You see, for every shameful thought or act we have committed or that others have committed against us, there exists a supernatural provision and replacement. We shout in the face of obstacles, knowing that somehow, someway, God will sustain and strengthen us. Our faith can grab hold of desolation and produce transformation. Don't limit yourself to what makes sense or what exists in the natural! God desires more for us than we can ask or even think.

So, when you lie down at night, ask our loving Father to cast off the broken and fill in every low place. Let the Holy Spirit minister to you as you go to sleep. "For He gives to His beloved even in his sleep" (Psalm 127:2).

Verbal Declarations

Declaring, or saying what God says about me, is something I do throughout my day, and especially in the mirror while getting dressed. Declarations change my inner world to match God's. Speaking His Word aloud strengthens me and sets me straight. I find speaking declarations aloud so powerful that I've included them at the end of every chapter.

We must speak the words of God aloud! This practice builds an arsenal of weapons against the enemy. When self-talk turns to shame and condemnation, when thoughts replay well-worn messages of doubt, lies, and lack, I pull out my arsenal of truth:

I am the apple of God's eye, His beloved.

I am chosen of God, holy and dearly loved.

I am blessed going in, and I'm blessed coming out.

What's in your arsenal right now? When inner dialogue cycles into shame, condemnation, and lies, we are quoting somebody, but not God! That's right; we are quoting Satan and retweeting every shamefaced lie he ever whispered into our hearts.

If you grew up in a shaming culture, or if you find your self-talk and parenting full of shaming techniques, listen to what *New York Times* best-selling author Brene Brown—who has spent two decades studying courage, vulnerability, shame, and empathy—discovered in her research:

> *"We live in a world where most people still subscribe to the belief that shame is a good tool for keeping people in line. Not only is this wrong, but it's dangerous. Shame is highly correlated with addiction, violence, aggression, depression, eating*

disorders, and bullying. Researchers don't find
shame correlated with positive outcomes at all."[58]

Brown also acknowledges the tendency to repeat our up-bringing, "My good friend and colleague Robert Hilliker says, 'Shame started as a two-person experience, but as I got older, I learned how to do shame all by myself.'"[59]

We must speak the loving truths of God to reshape our inner dialogue. Declarations are one way of doing that. Romans 10 echoes this truth: "Faith comes by hearing and hearing by the word of God." To have faith in God's goodness, I must hear His words coming out of my mouth. If your heart believes what you say, then say good things!

I often say, "Shame is overrated." It's a funny way to catch someone's attention, but it's true. Shame is overrated. Let's not partner with it in any way because "…those who hopefully wait for Me will not be put to shame" (Isaiah 49:23). I speak this verse out loud whenever I feel ashamed of myself—my looks, performance, relationships.

Faith is voice-activated, so I say the following declarations aloud during shame-inducing situations: "God will not put to shame those who hopefully wait on Him!" "Jesus, I'm looking to You right now to fill me, and I say, 'Get out' to any feelings of shame in this situation."

Declarations are an intentional, mindful practice, my friend. Wait on God, speak His truth, and proclaim His gracious loving-kindness! It will change your internal environment and tear down obstacles to gracious living.

Accountability with a Friend

Because we are social creatures, working on our graciousness is so much more effective if we do it with a friend. When I was in seminary, one of my pastoral classes required us to share personal reflections with a small group of classmates. I had to write about a conversation that left me with dissatisfaction. Reading my description, the small group gave feedback on cues I may have missed and ways to improve my understanding.

What an eye-opening experience! I reported on an exchange when I felt utterly misunderstood. My classmates gently illuminated my enormous blind spot in that conversation. Looking through their thoughtful lens, my confusion dissipated, and I made huge strides into gracious living through that exercise.

Hebrews 12:1-2 states, "Therefore, since we have so great a cloud of witnesses surrounding us, let us also lay aside every encumbrance and the sin which so easily entangles us, and let us run with endurance the race that is set before us, fixing our eyes on Jesus, the author and perfecter of faith, who for the joy set before Him endured the cross, despising the shame, and has sat down at the right hand of the throne of God."

Look at what we need to lay aside: sins and encumbrances. Think about it this way: you could run a race in strappy black heels, but those shoes would be an encumbrance! Carrying shame, sadness, and fear are encumbrances. With the help of the Holy Spirit, let's invest the time in laying them down.

Did Jesus lay aside sin? No, as He was sinless, but He did lay aside the sins committed against Him. So, let's look at that verse again. Do not only lay aside every encumbrance and sin, but also every sin committed against us and every harmful act encumbering us. Lay them at the feet of Jesus, who knows all about our pain. Run a steady race with eyes fixed on Him and know you have a great cloud of witnesses supporting you.

Our blind spots usually come to light during those close moments with girlfriends. As gentle, godly women, we hold space for each other and lend our vantage points to identify encumbrances we can't see on our own.

The Bread and the Cup

Communion, remembering Jesus through the bread and the cup, is something I do almost every day to align my heart with His. Communion is an alignment practice. I come to Him most mornings, balancing, organizing, sorting my heart and mind with what I understand of His.

> *"The Lord Jesus, in the night in which He was betrayed took bread; and when He had given thanks, He broke it and said, 'This is My body, which is for you; do this in remembrance of Me.' In the same way He took the cup also after supper, saying, 'This cup is the new covenant in My blood; do this, as often as you drink it, in remembrance of Me.' For as often as you eat this bread and drink the cup, you proclaim the Lord's death until He comes.'"* (1 Corinthians 11:23-26).

What happens when I "proclaim the Lord's death" by eating the communion meal? Through a physical act of eating the bread and drinking the cup, I'm actively remembering and appropriating. "In the night He was betrayed, He gave thanks" reminds me that in the darkest moments of life exists an opportunity for gratitude and surrender. And out of those deep, dark nights comes a healing provision.

When I read the words, "This is my body broken for you," I remember that His broken body purchased my healing. I embrace the words, "By His stripes I am healed," and I remember that cruel payment when I eat the bread. I ache with the realization that He was torn so that disease wouldn't tear me up. When I drink the cup, I drink the new covenant in His blood.

I remember that "without shedding of blood, there is no for-giveness" (Hebrews 9:22). As the drink stings my throat, I am reminded that His blood spilled out to buy me freedom from sin and a pathway to wholeness.

Could I remember all of this by reading my Bible during my quiet time? Of course, and I do. However, Jesus, the least tradition-oriented guy ever, said that when I enjoy the tradition of a communion meal, I am intentionally remembering and honoring Him. I am physically, mentally, and spiritually proclaiming the beautiful sacrifice He made on the cross.

I don't think Jesus advocated symbolic memory games in this meal. Pastor Beni Johnson writes:

> *"In Exodus, God had the Israelites kill a lamb and put the blood over their doors, signaling to the Spirit of God to pass by without harming the family inside…The physical lamb's blood didn't save them; the will of God saved them. But the families that participated in this prophetic act were revealing a heart submitted to God. The lamb's blood was a prophetic act that each family did in order to align themselves with God's will and alert the spirit realm as to whom they belonged. When Jesus led the disciples through Communion during their Passover meal together, He was creating and modeling a prophetic act that believers could continue implementing. He was giving us a way to align ourselves with Heaven and bring Heaven's reality to earth."*[60]

My friends, this strategic remembering positions me to contain the goodness God has poured into my life. Communion replaces bitterness, unforgiveness, shame, and fear and replaces it with His great love.

Just as painting white lines in a parking lot helps everyone find their space, I hope the five practices of forgiving, filling, declaring, sharing, and communion help you find your heart's space with God. We aren't built to carry the weight of sin, whether it's ours or someone else's. I've been surprised by what God has prompted me to forgive and how much drag these things had on my soul. My friend, through forgiving, filling, declaring, sharing, and communing, I hope you find your burden lifted and your friendship with Him deepened.

Is removing obstacles to gracious living a "one and done" process? Although some battles win decisive victories, others take time. We may work through forgiveness and shame to arrive at a fresh level of comfort and freedom, only to reveal there's more work ahead. Like peeling an onion, we may strip off fear, hurt, bitterness, pride—and other obstacles to gracious living—only to discover other layers of pain.

It's helpful to remember that God's goals for us are always relational. He's lovingly carrying us as these hurts and fears peel away to reveal our real identity. While everyday life erects obstacles to gracious living, we overcome them by having patterns in place. God's amazing love dispels fear and hurt.

Meaningful Dialogue

This chapter may stir painful memories. Proceed with gentleness.

1. Take a moment to discuss the parable in Matthew 18:23-35. What part do you identify with, and what aspect is a struggle?

2. How are you doing at forgiving yourself and others?

3. How have you experienced the Holy Spirit resurfacing and filling your life, especially in the areas that feel low or needful?

4. Where do you need to take an active role in making declarations of faith to strengthen your life?

5. Has communion been a significant experience for you? If not, how can you increase its influence on your spiritual journey?

Declarations for Gracious Living

Jesus continually gives me peace. (2 Thessalonians 3:16)

I am forgiving myself and others because Christ has forgiven me. (Colossians 3:13)

I am accepted in the Beloved! I give praise for the grace of God. (Ephesians 1:6)

17

The Gracious Living Challenge

"Take pains with these things; be absorbed in them.
So that your progress will be evident to all."

1 TIMOTHY 4:15

As a young, single woman, I joined an adventurer's scu-
ba-diving trip. On one voyage, our boat floated 100 miles off
the coast of Cuba, where we slid into dark, tepid water to explore an underwater cave.

Sinking into that silent, pitch-black crevice, I was thankful
for every bit of illumination from my flashlight. We followed
the cave's jagged walls, descending slowly through a winding
pathway that gradually narrowed. Eventually, I had to take the
oxygen tank off my back and push it in front of me. I kept my
breathing slow and steady to push down my rising panic.

Just when I couldn't have felt more uncomfortable, my fellow divers decided to fully experience our situation by turning off their lights! Hesitantly, I turned off mine as well, and in the depths of that pitch-black darkness, emotions flooded my mind. My first thought was *I'm forty feet underwater in a cave 100 miles from anything!* But my next thought was profound: "If I dwell in the remotest part of the sea, even there Your hand will lead me, and Your right hand will lay hold of me" (Psalm 139:9a-10).

You see, God instantly brought up a psalm I had read that morning, reassuring me of His presence, no matter how dark my circumstances. It was a moment I'll never forget. I was relieved to turn our flashlights back on and swim on to a broader space, but the peace I felt from God buoyed my soul.

Light That Shines Brighter

God's nearness is especially tender in dark, uncertain times. But light from another adventurer is also deeply cherished. It's a light that darkness cannot comprehend, a light that creates warmth and cheer with the smallest of gestures.

I remember a difficult season immediately after my college graduation. Without two dimes to rub together, I only had one can of Campbell's soup in my cabinet and no idea what to do when that was gone. Out of the blue, my college roomie's parents, who lived nearby, arrived at my door with a bag full of groceries. It was like a warm light in a dark cave. Those groceries were a gracious and thoughtful gesture that increased my hope and reminded me that I was not alone.

I still tenderly remember that graciousness, even though it happened more than thirty years ago. Nowadays, I don't need gifts of groceries or any material things to lighten my days, but I do need love, affirmation, encouragement, and purpose—as do you and every person you encounter! We all need reminders of God's purpose for our lives and the tremendous love that wraps around us every day. We all need to be treated with respect and kindness. We all long for a gracious culture.

In John 9:5, right before He healed the sight of a man born blind, Jesus said, "I am the light of the world." Jesus was defining Himself as the answer to this man's problem.

Jesus also defined the identity of His disciples when He proclaimed, "You are the light of the world. A city set on a hill cannot be hidden, nor does anyone light a lamp and put it under a basket, but on the lampstand, and it gives light to all who are in the house" (Matthew 5:14-15).

Your beautiful life cannot be hidden, my friend! And because you are the light of God's great love, you have an inherent purpose—to give light to all who are in the house.

Jesus concluded his disciple's identification with this admonition: "Let your light shine before men in such a way that they may see your good works and glorify your Father who is in heaven" (Matthew 5:16). You see, the ultimate purpose for gracious living is not that people will think better of us, but that they will think better of God.

Since I became a Christ-follower in 1978, I've read the Scriptures (God's love letters) almost every day. I can't believe how little I've memorized! I can't get past the feeling of only scratching the surface of His spectacular friendship, wisdom, and love. When I recently saw this quote from C.S. Lewis' *Chronicles of Narnia,* it perfectly fit my present season in Christ:

> *"Lucy woke out of the deepest sleep you can imagine, with the feeling that the voice she liked best in the world had been calling her name."*[61]

You see, every day I go about my life with a delicious sensation that the Holy Spirit is not just speaking to me and guiding my actions. He is also tenderly loving me, dancing with me, and singing to me. I feel full, complete, and deeply loved. It's a sensation I long to share with others.

When I get up in the morning to make my son's breakfast, it's for love. I'm loving him and praying that God's love extends through the pancakes and the backrub.

When I shop the aisles of a grocery store, I'm asking the Holy Spirit, "Is there anyone here who needs a word from You, a reminder of Your love?" And I'm nervous and excited when He points someone out to me. I get to show His love for that person. And sure, it's weird sometimes, but so what?

I often think about a delightful young man I met at a Cal Poly retreat who shared how lost and sinful he felt until, one day, in a park in Budapest, a man approached him and shared the gospel through broken English and Google translate. That young man gave his heart to the Lord that day and is growing in his love and obedience to Christ, along with his campus fellowship friends. His light shines because that man in Budapest let God's light shine through him.

That's the Holy Spirit loving us and loving through us—if we are willing to participate. Throughout my day, the Holy Spirit brings people to mind who need prayer or an encouraging email. So many times, I've sent a prayer or a Scripture to someone, and they have replied, "You have no idea how much I needed to hear this today!" And they are right. I don't have any idea, but my loving friend, the Holy Spirit, knows.

God sends me neighbors, salespeople, maintenance workers, and many others— all of them need an encounter with the living light of God, who happens to live inside of me. At my house this year, I've prayed for my plumber to receive sight back in his eye, and he did! I've studied Scripture with a Jewish HVAC salesperson, shared Bible verses and prayer with a repair tech, a landscaper, and pretty much anyone who rings my doorbell!

Anyone who dials my phone number is greeted by my "verse of the day," which honestly is more like the verse of the month because I forget to change it. The staff at my children's dentist office have confessed that they call my number frequently just to hear the Scripture and blessing. It's so fun sharing the light and love of God with everyone!

And speaking of light, half the time my iPhone flashlight is on in my back pocket! What am I saying? I'm a total dork. I'm just a middle-aged woman who was radically saved by Jesus and never got over it!

I have years of a love relationship built on trust and experience. I've seen prayers answered, bodies healed, demons cast out, love and purpose released, and hopping good times in worship. I've also seen prayers not answered, and bodies not healed, and dry and difficult seasons extend far too long. But I've tasted and seen that the Lord is good.

Gracious living is walking in His love, seeing with His eyes, and loving with His heart. Are you willing to partner with the beautiful work of the Holy Spirit to extend your hand in friendship, service, and love? Proverbs 4:18 tells us, "But the path of the righteous is like the light of dawn that shines brighter and brighter until the full day."

Your path of gracious living will be like the sun rising in the morning—your joy, generosity, and love will only increase! You've picked up insights as you've read this book. You've thoughtfully considered your impact in the world. Now, I want to challenge you to embrace three core principles of walking out the gracious life.

• **Let the Lord fully love you.** It takes time, focus, and quieting down, but don't settle for a passionless marriage with God. Receive His love. Let Him change you from the inside out. Jesus said He came to seek and to save the lost (Luke 19:10) The Greek word for save is sozo, and it means to save, heal, deliver, and make whole. Jesus didn't die a painful death on the cross to have a nodding acquaintance with you. He desires a closeness beyond your wildest imagination! This relationship is the fountainhead of all graciousness. This bond is our source for gracious giving, gracious living, and gracious sustaining.

Allow God's presence to infiltrate every part of your life. Receive His relationship that not only saves you for eternity, but also heals your brokenness, delivers you from an enemy seeking your destruction, and makes you whole.

• **Give away what you've got.** If God answered a prayer of yours today, tell somebody about it. If He has blessed and prospered you, share it so He can use you to lift someone higher. If God released peace into your heart and mind, be peaceful wherever you go.

The beauty of gracious living shines from the heart of one who loves sharing all the goodness of God. Paul wrote, "Blessed be the God and Father of our Lord Jesus Christ, the Father of mercies and God of all comfort, who comforts us in all our affliction so that we will be able to comfort those who are in any affliction with the comfort with which we ourselves are comforted by God" (2 Corinthians 1:3-4).

Gracious living is taking the comfort that God provides you and sharing it in comforting others. It's that simple! A friend of mine has experienced God's hand healing her marriage in beautiful ways. She delights in sharing her hopefulness when she meets another woman struggling with marriage. Give away whatever goodness, blessings, and favor you've received. Don't let the blessings stop with you!

• **Create a culture where you want to live.** Be the thermostat that sets the temperature in your world. Everywhere Jesus went during His time on earth, love and purpose followed. People realized their worth in His presence. They discovered the joy of living with intention. They witnessed what love looked like.

Creating a gracious culture can be disruptive. Sometimes, I feel like an oddity when I travel. I bring my Bible to breakfast and linger over it with endless cups of coffee. Because of this habit, I've been able to encourage and pray for waitstaff around the world. It has become my life's goal to create a culture that emanates graciousness, honor, beauty, compassion, and love.

An experience I had in Avignon, France, with a hotel manager reminds me of culture creation. My daughter, Brooke, and I were traveling. On our way out for the night, we asked the hotel manager if she knew of a good place for live music. She said there was none we would like. But Brooke and I found a rocking little place with a terrible band, and we recorded a quick video of us dancing with an old Frenchman.

When Brooke and I saw the hotel manager the next morning, we laughingly shared the video from the previous night. The conversation that emerged was clearly from God.

The manager looked at us intently and said, "I have never seen this before – you are a mother and daughter, yes? You are so loving with each other." Then she asked, "What is your secret?"

I told her straight out: it's Jesus! We had a long discussion about how Christ can change us from the inside out and bring His love and peace into our homes and families. The woman was pregnant with her first child, and Brooke and I had the honor to place our hands on her stomach and pray a blessing on her child.

Love, in the words of 1 Corinthians 13, can be patient and kind, because it's not about us; it's about the other person. We can create this gracious culture of love and honor, just as Jesus did with prostitutes and publicans alike, because our focus is on the giving rather than receiving.

As I'm writing, Kanye West's album, "Jesus is King," just dropped. I have listened to it on repeat all week. I've studied the lyrics. I've smiled at lines about not having to "peek over" heaven's gates, and then cried over words about Jesus being the King of kings.

Seeing Kanye's public transformation and bold proclamation of the gospel reminded me of this: Who we are matters. We can possess gazillions of dollars but be empty without the friendship of Christ. It matters that we are gracious and loving. It impacts everyone around us that we hold peace and walk in gentleness. It matters, my friend.

Kanye's example has been like a shockingly cold splash of water to the face. I pray for him as a bold Christ-follower—that he will continue to climb even though a lot of people seek to bring him down. I could look at many Christian pop artists and complain that their lyrics hardly reveal Christ compared to Kanye's bold proclamation that Jesus is King. However, I've also had to look in the mirror and confront my lack of boldness and clarity. This acknowledgment is not about shame; it's about conviction. We all long to live a life full of adventure and impact. Don't let anyone talk you down from the heights you want to climb!

Dear friend, don't give up. Don't take your foot off the gas as you grow toward gracious living. As you make space for others to rest in your graciousness, you may never know who you impact and how much.

We all occasionally travel on the quick-and-easy path of impatience, irritation, and brusque behavior. But we also know God calls us to more. I don't think I had a graciousness about me in my thirties. I was growing into it, but my hope for young gals today is that they will hold hands with the Holy Spirit earlier in their lives. Our world so desperately needs women to walk with God in such a profound way that cultures of honor, compassion, and love naturally spring up.

Continue to Shine

Luke 15 tops my list of Bible chapters that demonstrate gracious living. I could spend hours analyzing it! Precious pearls of wisdom and insight are scattered all over this chapter. It begins in the context of tax collectors and sinners wanting to hang out with Jesus. He was chilling with the rowdy folk at their favorite café, and the religious leaders were appalled.

In response, Jesus told three parables to illustrate God's heart for people. The first two parables, the lost sheep and the lost coin, represent God's perseverance in finding those separated from Him—and all of heaven celebrating their return to His care. But we don't quite catch the gracious and forgiving nature of God until the third parable. The prodigal son is a lesson in gracious living.

At first, I questioned why the parable didn't exclude the older son and merely relate the story of the son who wandered away. But the contrast between the father's responses to the prodigal and the older brother is pure gold. The father (representing God) graciously fulfilled the younger son's premature request for his inheritance. To ensure that God's gracious love was fully displayed, Jesus made the point that the son "squandered his estate with loose living" (Luke 15:13) and "devoured your wealth with prostitutes" (Luke 15:30).

Jesus' parable went on to say the son stooped so low as to feed pigs as his occupation. To the Jewish audience, not only was this son brash, disrespectful, and immoral, he was also disgustingly unclean in both the physical and religious sense.

In spite of all this, when the father (God) saw his son in the distance, he tossed dignity aside and sprinted out to meet him. Where was the lecture? The condescending "process" of restoration? There was only unbridled affection and celebration for the son's return. "Quickly bring out the best robe and put it on him, and put a ring on his hand and sandals on his feet; and bring the fattened calf, kill it, and let us eat and celebrate; for this son of mine was dead and has come to life again; he was lost but found. And they began to celebrate" (Luke 15:22-24).

God restores our dignity, authority, and inherent worth with His acceptance and grace. That should propel you and I to stand up and holler, "Hallelujah!"

Sadly, our responses may more closely mirror that of the older brother. Upon hearing of the prodigal's return and the father's hearty celebration, the older brother was angry and refused to participate. He bitterly recounted how hard he had worked, how precisely he followed commands, and that he never felt celebrated himself.

The father answered, "All that is mine is yours." (Luke 15:31) Just like us, the older brother was an owner but not a possessor. Legally, all that the Father held was for him. It was his by right, but he did not possess it experientially. We cognitively know that we inherit all things through Christ; we have His credit card! But do we often walk in His joy, peace, love, and graciousness?

If we want to see change, it must begin within us. I must change myself; you must change yourself. If we want joy to bubble in our homes, it must first live within us. If we seek an honoring culture, honor must grow inside us.

I'm not asking you to white-knuckle your way through gracious living. Just plant little seeds each day that will bring you a harvest in the future. If you plant an apple seed, you'll eventually get apples. You are telling your tomorrow what you want it to become every time you plant a seed. If you plant kindness, goodness, beauty, honor, and joy, you will soon walk in fields of those traits. (Similarly, if you deposit tiny seeds of irritation, immorality, cursing, and greed, you'll live that desolate harvest.)

I challenge you to cultivate gracious seeds in your family, workplace, church, and friendships. Soon, you will see tiny green shoots sprouting forth. These little blades of progress may appear as easy laughter in your home, affection with your children, significant conversations with strangers, gracious words with coworkers, and loving exchanges at church. Every day brings a fresh surrender to God's wonderful plan.

Would you join me in committing our hopes for gracious living to God with a declaration of Scripture? The best, my friend, is yet to come.

> *"Now to Him who is able to do far more abun-*
> *dantly beyond all that we ask or think, according*
> *to the power that works within us, to Him be*
> *the glory in the church and in Christ Jesus to all*
> *generations forever and ever. Amen."* (Ephesians
> 3:20-21)

Meaningful Dialogue

1. What act of graciousness has touched you recently? How did it impact you?

2. Reflect on Jesus' proclamation "You are the light of the world." When do you feel that is true of you?

3. How are you growing into gracious living? Do specific situations come to mind?

4. How do the three parables in Luke 15 (the lost sheep, the lost coin, the prodigal son) shape your view of gracious living?

5. What is your plan to expand your graciousness?

Declarations for Gracious Living

I am the light of the world! (Matthew 5)

Heaven is cheering for me! (Luke 15)

God is doing more for me than I can even imagine. (Ephesians 3)

Meaningful Dialogue Questions

PART ONE: REACHING IN

Chapter 1: Women Who Create

1. Describe an experience that softened you. What did God reveal to you during that time?

2. What negative environments could you change to create positive spaces?

3. When have you felt someone was trying to fix you? Have you caught yourself trying to fix others or change their behavior?

4. Where do you need the Holy Spirit to come alive in your life? You can ask for the Spirit's help, knowing that His voice will lovingly bring you closer to God.

5. Are you holding anything back from God? Is there any area of your life that you are afraid to hear what He has to say?

Chapter 2: A Touch of Self-Grace

1. Which areas of your life are the hardest to show yourself grace?

2. What Scriptures could you speak, or even memorize, that strengthen your identity in Christ? What are truths about you, as a believer, in Scripture?

3. What are lies, whispered by the enemy, that hurt or impede your walk with God? How can you rebuke that line of thinking and replace it with truth?

4. What phrases and self-talk can you practice in your everyday thoughts and conversations to bring about positive change?

5. Whether you have been around church for years or are brand new to the God scene, what are ways you can wholeheartedly enter into the love of Jesus?

Chapter 3: The Soul of Friendship

1. Do you have a friend with whom you share a deep commitment and relationship? How did you get there?

2. How have you exercised forgiveness in your friendships? Is there anyone you need to be reconciled with now?

3. Are you envious of the friendship described between Jonathan and David, or is loyalty a strong characteristic in your friends?

4. What are ways your friendships could grow in closeness, honor, and commitment?

Chapter 4: Living in the Love Lab

1. How are you pursuing a friendship with your spouse?

2. Where do you struggle to be gracious in your marriage?

3. Do any areas of your life need better boundaries to ensure a stronger marriage?

4. Do you have regular date nights and "state of the union" meetings? How about regular prayer times together? Share how these experiences strengthen your marriage bond.

Chapter 5: Adulting With Grace

1. What do you appreciate about your upbringing? What are the ways you can express your affection and gratitude toward your parents?

2. When do you need God's strength in your relationship with your parents?

3. How do you communicate healthy boundaries with your parents? Is this difficult?

4. Where does there need to be healing and forgiveness in your relationship with your parents?

5. Is honor a part of your family culture? If not, how could you incorporate it into your relationship?

Chapter 6: The Value of Children

1. What are your memories of being cherished as a child? Does this impact your parenting now?

2. When is it difficult to value and enjoy your children? How can you change your mindset in those moments?

3. How do you engage God in your parenting? Is prayer important to your relationship with your children?

4. What are the habits you need to break that are negatively impacting your family?

5. What are practical ways your family could enjoy a sabbath?

Chapter 7: Caregiving & Receiving

1. How have you have received care and given care? Describe what that was like for you.

2. How can you rely on the Holy Spirit while caring for others? Do you sense a partnership with Him, or do you feel all alone in caregiving?

3. How can you encourage yourself and others involved in caregiving?

4. Because this process sometimes involves loss, is there anyone you need to forgive or release to God?

PART 2: REACHING OUT

Chapter 8: Churchy Girls

1. Think about your history with church. Have there been positive or negative experiences that shape how you approach church?

2. How can you bring a more gracious atmosphere into your church?

3. Has your church experience been touched by judging or criticizing? How do you combat these attitudes?

4. What examples come to mind of gracious people within your church who love and serve others?

5. What are ways you can participate in bringing God's glorious church to your community of friends, neighbors, and coworkers?

Chapter 9: The Welcome Mat

1. When do you feel the need to look like the picture-perfect host? How does that feel for you? How does your perfection mindset make your family and guests feel?

2. What was Mary's mindset as she hosted Jesus as contrasted to Martha's? Where do you resonate on the Mary-Martha scale?

3. Who could you bless with hospitality? What stops you from hosting others?

4. What does it look like to welcome the Holy Spirit's presence into your home and your hosting?

Chapter 10: Working at It

1. How do you correlate your Christian beliefs at work with your thoughts, actions, and behaviors?

2. What is the atmosphere of your company? Who impacts it positively or negatively? How could you be the thermostat for your work atmosphere?

3. How is prayer incorporated into your work life?

4. How are you at receiving and expressing gratitude at work? What could you improve?

5. Do your coworkers know about your faith? Are there significant ways you can share who Christ is to you?

Chapter 11: A Mentor's Vision

1. Explore the ways Jesus mentored His disciples. How could you use His methods in your life?

2. Have you been mentored at church or work? Have you ever been a mentor for someone else? Describe your experiences.

3. What do you consider obstacles to mentorship? Do you have any concerns about time, relationships, or Bible knowledge?

4. How can you keep your guidance positive and free from judgment?

5. Is there someone God deposited on your heart to mentor? Pray about this now!

Chapter 12: Stranger Things

1. What are small and large gestures of kindness you can show to strangers? Do you have any recent examples?

2. How have strangers shown grace or kindness to you? How did that feel?

3. How can you adopt a lifestyle of actively looking to bless others as you go about your day?

4. Do spiritual conversations come up in your interactions? How do you transition from chit-chat to something of depth?

Chapter 13: Social Media Reclaim

1. What part of social media feels like a drag on your time and positivity?

2. Have you discovered ways to bless and encourage others through social media? What does it look like?

3. How do you set yourself up for success in online activities so that you have no regrets around anything said or time spent?

4. How much are comparison and jealousy a struggle in your social media experience?

5. Do you find yourself feeling angry and agitated after being online? Or sad and feeling less than everyone else? How do you process this and safeguard against it?

Chapter 14: Open Hands

1. Was generosity modeled to you growing up? Does anyone in your life stand out to you as a compelling example of a graciously generous person?

2. Brainstorm some examples of generosity in the life of Jesus. How can you emulate these?

3. How do you plan generosity into your budget of time, talent, or treasure?

4. Is generosity an integral part of your walk with God now? Does giving or advocacy present a struggle in some ways?

PART THREE: WALKING YOUR PATH

Chapter 15: Beautiful Boundaries

1. Where in your life do you find it challenging to hold boundaries?

2. Do you ever struggle with your needs seeming to be less important than the needs of others?

3. What are gracious ways you have set up boundaries?

4. What relationship in your life needs more honor and grace extended rather than limits? Do you feel called to give and serve in any particular area?

5. What is the hardest part of living with boundaries? What's the best part?

Chapter 16: Overcoming Obstacles

1. Take a moment to discuss the parable in Matthew 18:23-35. What part do you identify with, and what aspect is a struggle?

2. How are you doing at forgiving yourself and others?

3. How have you experienced the Holy Spirit resurfacing and filling your life, especially in the areas that feel low or needful?

4. Where do you need to take an active role in making declarations of faith to strengthen your life?

5. Has communion been a significant experience for you? If not, how can you increase its influence on your spiritual journey?

Chapter 17: The Gracious Living Challenge

1. What act of graciousness has touched you recently? How did it impact you?

2. Reflect on Jesus' proclamation, "You are the light of the world." When do you feel that is true for you?

3. How are you growing into gracious living? Do specific situations come to mind?

4. How do the three parables in Luke 15 (the lost sheep, the lost coin, the prodigal son) shape your view of gracious living?

5. What is your plan to expand your graciousness?

Declarations for Gracious Living

Copy and post these declarations where you can read and memorize them.

Creating Positive Atmosphere

As the eyes of servants look to their master, so my eyes look to You, O God! (Psalms 123:2)

The Lord leads me in the way I should go. (Isaiah 48:17)

I am brimming with righteousness and peace and joy in the Holy Spirit! (Romans 14:17)

Self-Grace

Whoever calls on the name of the Lord will be saved, healed, delivered, and made whole. (Romans 10:13)

God has loved me with an everlasting love. (Jeremiah 31:3)

I take every thought captive to the obedience of Christ, and I destroy every lofty thing raised against the knowledge of God. (2 Corinthians 10:5)

Friendship

I am a friend who sticks closer than a brother. (Proverbs 18:24)

I am rooted and grounded in love; therefore, I can give and receive love from my friends. (Ephesians 3:17)

Whatever is true, honorable, pure, and lovely, I dwell on these things, and they are being reproduced in my life. (Philippians 4:8)

Marriage

I am my beloved's, and he is mine. (Song of Solomon 6:3)

I rejoice in hope for my marriage. (Romans 12:12)

I persevere through every trial in my marriage. (Romans 12:12)

I am devoted to prayer for my marriage. (Romans 12:12)

My marriage is a prophetic picture of how Christ loves the church. (Ephesians 5:25)

Adulting

I bless my mother and father in Jesus' name! (Matthew 19:19)

God knew me before I was in the womb. (Psalm 139)

He has set me apart and appointed me to this life. (Jeremiah 1:5)

My inheritance is beautiful. (Psalm 16:6)

Parenting

My children are a gift from the Lord! (Psalm 127:3)

I am patient. I am kind. I am not easily provoked. I can bear all things, believe all things, hope all things and endure all things because of the love of God in me. (1 Corinthians 13:4-7)

I honor the sabbath and call it a delight. (Isaiah 58:13-14)

Caregiving & Receiving

I have all the strength I need! I can keep on doing all things through Christ who keeps on strengthening me.
(Philippians 4:13)

I have peace unlike what the world gives. (John 14:27)

I have perfect peace because my mind is set on God.
(Isaiah 26:3)

God knows the plans He has for me and those plans are for my good. (Jeremiah 29:11)

Church

The kingdom of God is at hand. I will be about His work.
(Mark 1:15)

I will let my light shine to bring glory to God. (Matthew 5:16)

I am a royal priesthood, a people for God's own possession!
(1Peter 2:9)

Hosting

I entertain angels by being hospitable. (Hebrews 13:2)

I have perfect peace because I trust in You. (Isaiah 26:3)

My home is a gift from You. I am generous with all that I have.
(James 1:17)

Workplace

I am the light of the world! I bring wisdom, joy, and peace everywhere I go. (Matthew 5:14)

I do my work heartily as unto the Lord. (Colossians 3:23)

I give thanks for all things, for this is the will of God in Christ Jesus. (1 Thessalonians 5:18)

Mentoring

I have discovered treasures in Christ, and I will not hide them! (Colossians 2:3)

"Now we who are strong ought to bear the weaknesses of those without strength and not just please ourselves." (Romans 15:1)

I imitate God as a beloved child. I walk in love just as Christ loved. (Ephesians 5:1)

Strangers

I trust in the Lord in all my ways, and I don't lean on my understanding. (Proverbs 3:5)

God is always speaking. I partner with Him to release truth, grace, and beauty. (1 Peter 4:11)

I am enthusiastic about doing good works. (1 Peter 3:13)

God created me for good works which He has already prepared for me to do. (Ephesians 2:10)

Social Media

I have made a covenant with my eyes. (Job 31:1)

The words of my mouth and the meditations of my heart are pure before God. (Psalms 19:14)

God is teaching me to number my days so that I can present to Him a heart of wisdom. (Psalms 90:12)

Generosity

I am blessed coming in and blessed going out!
(Deuteronomy 28:6)

I have all that I need for life and godliness. (2 Peter 1:3)

I am a good steward of my time, talent and treasure. I abound in gracious works! (2 Corinthians 8:7)

Boundaries

I do good to all people for whatever I sow I also reap.
(Galatians 6:7,10)

I am God's workmanship, created in Christ Jesus for good works.
(Ephesians 2:10)

I watch over my heart and steward my life with all diligence.
(Proverbs 4:23)

Obstacles

Jesus continually gives me peace. (2 Thessalonians 3:16)

I am forgiving myself and others because Christ has forgiven me. (Colossians 3:13)

I am accepted in the Beloved! I give praise for the grace of God.
(Ephesians 1:6)

Challenge

I am the light of the world! (Matthew 5)

Heaven is cheering for me! (Luke 15)

God is doing more for me than I can even imagine.
(Ephesians 3)

Scripture Index

Chapter 1 Women Who Create

Psalm 126:5, Matthew 23:25, 1 Corinthians 12,14, Luke 10:25-37, Isaiah 49:6, 1 John 4:19, Psalm 103:8, Psalm 123:2, Isaiah 48:17, Romans 14:17

Chapter 2 A Touch of Self-Grace

Psalm 139:14, Psalm 34:10, Proverbs 28:1, Romans 8:38-39, 1 Samuel 3:19, Romans 10:13, Jeremiah 31:3, 2 Corinthians 10:5

Chapter 3 The Soul of Friendship

1 Samuel 18:1, 1 Samuel 20:30-31, 1 Samuel 18- 2 Samuel 9, 1 Samuel 19:4-5, 1 Corinthians 13:5-7, 1 Samuel 18:4, Proverbs 18:24, Ephesians 3:17, Philippians 4:8

Chapter 4 Living in the Love Lab

Song of Solomon 2:16, Nehemiah 1:4,2:4,4:9,5:19,6:9,14, 13:31, 4:14, 6:3,13, Genesis 2:24, Nehemiah 1:8-9, Romans 12:10, Psalm 19:14, Ephesians 5:25, 28-33, Ecclesiastes 14:9-12, Song of Solomon 6:3, Romans 12:2, Ephesians 5:25

Chapter 5 Adulting with Grace

Proverbs 1:8, Jeremiah 1:5, Ecclesiastes 4:9-10, 1 Peter 4:8, Psalm 17:7-8, Psalm 90:2, Psalm 101:2, Psalm 103:1-5, Exodus 20:8-11, Mark 2:27-28, Psalm 127:3, 1 Corinthians 13:4-7, Isaiah 58:13-14

Chapter 6 Kid Value

Proverbs 13:1, Proverbs 10:1, Matthew 4:18-22, Matthew 12:48, Matthew 19:18-19, Matthew 15:4, Ephesians 6:1-3, Hebrews 12:11, John 19:26-27, Colossians 3:23-24, Jeremiah 1:5, Psalm 16:6

Chapter 7 Caregiving & Receiving

Psalm 42:8, Psalm 86:7, Romans 12:18, Isaiah 26:3, Exodus 18:14-27, James 5:17, 2 Corinthians 1:4, Philippians 2:3-4, John 14:27, Matthew 11:28, Philippians 4:13, John 14:27, Isaiah 26:3, Jeremiah 29:11

Chapter 8 Churchy Girls

1 Timothy 3:15, 1 Peter 2:9, Acts 20:28, Romans 12:16-17, Romans 12:10, Proverbs 18:21, Galatians 3:28, Matthew 11:28, 1 Peter 2:10-12, Matthew 13:24-30,36-43, Mark 1:15, Matthew 5:16, 1 Peter 2:9

Chapter 9 The Welcome Mat

Luke 5:29, 1 Peter 4:9, Luke 10:40-43, John 15:15, Luke 7:36-50, 2 Kings 4:18-37, 2 Kings 8:1-6, Titus 1:8, 1 Timothy 3:2, Hebrews 13:2, Matthew 25:35-36,40 Isaiah 26:3, James 1:17

Chapter 10 Working at It

Colossians 3:23, 2 Thessalonians 3:7-11, Proverbs 15:19, 22:28, 27:18, 12:18, 15:1, Titus 3:2, Jeremiah 29:7, Philippians 4:6-7, 1 Thessalonians 5:16-18, Proverbs 27:23, Colossians 3:23-24

Chapter 11 A Mentor's Vision

Isaiah 46:10, 1 Corinthians 4:15-17, Matthew 28:19-20, 2 Kings 7, Philippians 2:20-21, 1 Thessalonians 2:7-8, Romans 15:1, Ephesians 5:1

Chapter 12 Stranger Things

Matthew 25:35, Exodus 23:9, Malachi 3:5, Psalm 39:12, Psalm 68:6, Luke 13:21, Proverbs 3:5, 1 Peter 4:11, 1 Peter 3:13, Ephesians 2:10

Chapter 13 Social Media Reclaim

Psalm 19:14, 2 Timothy 3:2-5, Proverbs 6:27, Psalm 37:7, Psalm 37:3-6, Luke 11:43, 2 Timothy 3:7, Ephesians 4:29, Proverbs 17:4, Proverbs 6:20, Galatians 5:19, Proverbs 4:24-27, Hebrews 4:13, Job 31:1, Psalm 19:14, Psalm 90:10

Chapter 14 Open Hands

Psalm 37:21, Proverbs 3:9-10,27-28, Proverbs 11:25, 19:17, 13:23, 31:8-9, 31:20, Matthew 6:1-2, Leviticus 19, 2 Corinthians 9:6, Luke 6:38, 2 Corinthians 9:8, 2 peter 1:3, Psalm 34:10, Proverbs 11:25, Deuteronomy 28:6, 2 Peter 1:3, 2 Corinthians 8:7

Chapter 15 Overcoming Obstacles

2 Thessalonians 3:16, 1 Peter 5:7, John 15, Matthew 18:21-35, Ephesians 4:32, Colossians 3:13, 2 Corinthians 2:10-11, Luke 3:5, Isaiah 54:1,4, Psalm 127:2, Romans 10:17, Isaiah 49:23, Hebrews 12:1-2, 1 Corinthians 11:23-26

Chapter 16 Beautiful Boundaries

Galatians 6:2,5, Philippians 4:13, Isaiah 49:16, James 5:12, John 15:13, Philippians 1:9-10, Ephesians 2:10

Chapter 17 The Gracious Living Challenge

1 Timothy 4:15, Psalm 139:9-10, John 9:5, Matthew 5:14-16, Proverbs 4:18, Luke 19:10, 2 Corinthians 1:3-4, 1 Corinthians 13, Luke 15, Ephesians 3:20-21

Notes

Chapter 1: Women Who Create
1 Shawn Bolz, Translating God, Glendale, CA: ICreate Productions, 2015, 20.

Chapter 3: The Soul of Friendship
2 https://www.health.harvard.edu/mental-health/can-relation-ships-boost-longevity-and-well-being, accessed December 10, 2019.
3 https://www.inc.com/video/tim-ferriss/decision-making-if-its-not-hell-yeah-its-a-no.html, accessed December 10, 2019.

Chapter 4: Living in the Love Lab
4 John M. Gottman, *The Seven Principles for Making Marriage Work*, New York, New York: Harmony Books, 21.
5 Ibid, 202.

Chapter 5: Adulting with Grace
6 Deborah Tannen, *You're Wearing That? Understanding Mothers and Daughters in Conversation*, New York, NY: Ballatine Books, a division of Random House, Inc., 2006, 138-139.
7 Ibid, 59.
8 https://quoteinvestigator.com/2010/10/10/twain-father. Accessed December 10, 2019.
9 Tannen, 11, 34.
10 Some names in *Gracious Living* have been changed for privacy.
11 Tannen, 26.

Chapter 6: Investing in Kid Value
12 David Allen, *Getting Things Done*, New York, New York: Penguin Books, 2015.

Chapter 7: Caregiving & Receiving
13 Ibid.

Chapter 8: Churchy Girls
14 Ansel Post, *Way of Faith*, quoted in Frank Bartleman, Azusa Street, South Plainfield, N.J: Bridge Publishing, 1980, 61.
15 Jessica Smartt, *How to Introduce Your Child to Jesus* (Amazon digital services, 2014).
16 Bessel Van Der Kolk, *The Body Keeps the Score*, New York, NY: Penguin Books, 2014, 212.
17 Ibid, 212
18 Jessica Smartt, *Memory Making Mom*, Nashville, TN: Thomas Nelson, 2019, 74.

Chapter 9: The Welcome Mat
19 Bill Johnson, *Hosting the Presence*, Shippensburg, PA: Destiny Image Publishers, 2012, 170.

Chapter 10: Working at It
20 Gallup Study https://www.gallup.com/workplace/267743/why-millennials-job-hopping.aspx
21 Angela Duckworth, Grit: The Power of Passion and Perseverance, New York, NY: Scriber, 2016, 103.
22 Ibid, 91.
23 Ibid, 58.
24 Ibid, 91.
25 James M. Kouzes and Barry Z. Posner, The Leadership Challenge 4th Edition, San Francisco, CA: John Wiley & Sons, Inc., 2007, 302.
26 Ibid, 347.
27 Tim Ferris, Tools of Titans, Penguin Random House UK, 2016, 157.
28 Kouzes & Posner, 338.
29 Kouzes & Posner, 299.
30 Kouzes & Posner, 300.

Chapter 11: A Mentor's Vision
31 "Truth the Poet Sings" An anthology of Unity Poets.
32 Erin Seheult, "Generational Mentorship: What Millennial Mentees Want," https://www.questia.com/library/journal/1P3-4183593951/

generational-mentorship-what-millennial-mentees-want. Accessed
December 10, 2019.

33 Richard Kipling, "The Glory of the Garden," *A History of England,*
London: Oxford, 1911.

Chapter 12: Stranger Things

34 *passiton.com/inspirationalquotes/7239-the-greatest-good-you-can-
do-for-another-is-not.* Accessed April 15, 2020.

35 Henry Blackaby and Claude King, *Knowing God,* (Nashville, TN:
Lifeway, 1990), 77.

36 Edgar A. Guest, Poem "Faith," The Boston Globe, August 19, 1915,
(Boston, Massachusetts). As quoted in *Detroit Free Press,* page 10,
column 4. (Newspaper Archive).

37 https://www.translateen.com/quote/authors/lamine-pearlheart.
Accessed 1/02/2020.

Chapter 13: Social Media Reclaim

38 Karen Ehman, "What Matters Most," (Nashville, TN: LifeWay
Press, 2018), 149.

39 From "Life is Short," January 2016, *Paulgraham.com*

40 Douglas Kaine McKelvey, "Every Moment Holy" (Nashville, TN:
Rabbit Room Press, 2017), 159

Chapter 14: Open Hands

41 https://www.ted.com/talks/
bryan_stevenson_we_need_to_talk_about_an_injustice?language=en

Chapter 15: Beautiful Boundaries

42 Henry Cloud & John Townsend, *Boundaries,* Zondervan:
Michigan, 1992, 73.

43 Ibid, 161

44 Ibid, 158.

45 Ibid, 107.

46 Ibid, 199.

47 Lysa TerKeurst, *The Best Yes,* Thomas Nelson: Nashville, 2014, 55.

48 Cloud and Townsend, 102-103.

49 TerKeurst, 161.

50 Cloud and Townsend, 168.

51 Ibid, 110.

52 Ibid, 137.
53 TerKeurst, 5.

Chapter 16: Overcoming Obstacles

54 Bessel Van Der Kolk, M.D, "The Body Keeps the Score," Penguin Books, New York, New York: 2014, p. 223.
55 Jackson Browne, "Your Bright Baby Blues" The Pretender, Asylum Records, 1976.
56 Robert McGee, "Search for Significance," Life Support edition workbook, Lifeway, Nashville, TN: 1992, p. 134.
57 Ed M. Smith, "Theophostic Prayer Ministry Basic Seminar Manual," Campbellsville, KY: New Creation Publishing, 2005, 99.
58 Brene Brown, "Daring Greatly," Gotham Books, New York, New York: 2012, 72-73.
59 Ibid, 67.
60 Beni Johnson, "The Power of Communion," Destiny Image Publishers, Shippensburg, PA: 2019, 18-19.

Chapter 17: The Gracious Living Challenge

61 C. S. Lewis, "The Chronicles of Narnia, Prince Caspian," HarperCollins, New York, New York, 1956, 174.

Connect with Margaret Allen

Want to deepen your walk with Christ after reading *Gracious Living*? You'll find free resources and declarations for a gracious life at www.MargaretAllen.org. Each week, Margaret also posts encouraging words to guide your journey. Just click on "Mondays with Margaret."

You can connect with Margaret on Instagram *@MargaretAllen. GL* and Facebook/*Margaret Allen*.

To have Margaret speak at your next event, visit www. MargaretAllen.org, and complete the contact form at the bottom of the page.

Stay tuned for Margaret's upcoming book, *40 Days of Gracious Living*. This devotional, written with the feminine heart in mind, includes uplifting Scripture, words of encouragement, and biblical declarations for gracious living.

Connect with
Ivey Harrington Beckman

In the hands of a deft editor, words are magical seeds that spring to life and wrap the reader in the vibrancy of story.

Ivey Harrington Beckman provides book authors with in-depth editorial guidance to ensure superior content. To connect with Ivey, visit www.iveyharringtonbeckman.com, and click on the "Connect with Ivey" tab.